COMPARISON OF AUDIT METHODOLOGIES OF LARGE ACCOUNTING FIRMS

AMERICAN ACCOUNTING ASSOCIATION

The By-Laws of the American Accounting Association state that the first purpose of the Association shall be "to initiate, encourage, and sponsor research in accounting and to publish or aid in the publication of the results of research." In harmony with his objective, the publication of the Studies in Accounting Research is aimed at encouraging and publishing research. This series is an outgrowth of the research program initiated by the Association in 1965. Under this program research projects and authors are selected by the Director of Research, who is assisted by a Research Advisory Committee.

When the project is commissioned, the author is allowed maximum freedom in conducting research. The author is solely responsible for the procedures followed and the research conclusions.

This project was commissioned by William R. Kinney, Jr., Director of Research. The Research Advisory Committee for this project consisted of:

William L. Felix, Jr.	University of Arizona
Bart H. Ward	University of Oklahoma
Carl S. Warren	University of Georgia

COMPARISON OF AUDIT METHODOLOGIES OF LARGE ACCOUNTING FIRMS

by
Barry E. Cushing
and James K. Loebbecke
University of Utah

AMERICAN ACCOUNTING ASSOCIATION
1986

Library of Congress Catalog Card Number 85-073191
ISBN 0-86539-060-6
Printed in the United States of America

TABLE OF CONTENTS

ACKNOWLEDGMENTS

It would not have been possible to undertake a research project of this type without two things: financial resources and extensive cooperation. We take this opportunity to acknowledge and thank those institutions and persons who provided these essential ingredients to us.

Financial assistance was generously provided by the Peat, Marwick, Mitchell Foundation through their Research Opportunities in Auditing Program. Not only were funds provided, but also patience, which we greatly appreciate. Indirect financial assistance was provided by the University of Utah College of Business through the use of facilities and personnel. More important, the University of Utah encouraged us to undertake this project and supported our efforts through to its conclusion.

The extent of effort and cooperation we received from the participating firms and certain others was far more than we expected or consider "reasonable." We would like to thank each of these organizations, and particularly the individuals involved, by listing them below. We wish there was a more appropriate or ceremonious way to express our sincere and deep appreciation.

Our thanks to:

Jerry Serlin and Bob Mednick of Arthur Andersen & Co.
Herm Rosenman and Dick Gnospelius of Coopers & Lybrand
Jim Kirtland of Deloitte, Haskins & Sells and Gary Holstrum of the University of Southern California, formerly of Deloitte, Haskins & Sells
Mike Grobstein and Dick Hissam of Ernst & Whinney
Jim Ries and Bill Dent of Fox & Company
Ed Krebs, Ted Asner and Chuck Werner of Alexander Grant & Company
Ken Dirkes, Vern Johnson and Frank Caveney of Main Hurdman
Bob Elliott and John Willingham of Peat, Marwick, Mitchell & Co., and Dane Brooksher and Priscilla Patterson of the Peat, Marwick, Mitchell Foundation
Wally Pugh, Sherry Biggs and Ralph Hoffman of Price Waterhouse
Frank Pearlman and Harvey Moskowitz of Seidman & Seidman
John Mullarkey and Bob Kay of Touche Ross & Co.
Jack Broderick of Arthur Young & Company
Dave Landsittel and Jim Leisenring, Chairmen of the Auditing Standards Board, Phil Chenok, Bill Metzger, and Dan Guy of the AICPA, and Doug Carmichael of Baruch College of the City University of New York, formerly of the AICPA.

Barry E. Cushing
James K. Loebbecke

June, 1985

CHAPTER ONE

Introduction

Our purpose is to obtain a better understanding of the nature of auditing by analyzing the way in which it functions. (Mautz and Sharaf in *The Philosophy of Auditing*—1961)

Objectives of the Study

As a basis for their landmark work, Mautz and Sharaf pointed to the absence in the academic literature of a real understanding of how auditing is done. Although research has since been done on many aspects of the auditing process, most of this research has been normative rather than descriptive.[1] The few descriptive surveys that have been published have focused on specific parts of the auditing process, rather than on the process as a whole.[2] Accordingly, our understanding of the overall process by which actual audits are conducted is incomplete. This exploratory study is intended to increase our understanding of the auditing process.

Many of the larger accounting firms have implemented major changes in their auditing methodologies in the period since the mid-1970s. These changes have generally been toward greater structure or formalization of the firm's audit approach; i.e., toward recognition of the audit as an integrated *process*, not simply a collection of isolated procedures. The firms have had several motives for making these changes, including: 1) a need to implement a consistent approach across a large practice; 2) a need to control audit risk and audit costs more effectively; 3) a desire to enhance auditor-client communication; and 4) a desire to achieve a distinguishable image in the market place. Although the materials describing these audit methodologies are proprietary, some are shared outside the firm through presentations, public relations efforts, and work on American Institute of Certified Public Accountants (AICPA) projects.

With regard to this latter exposure, we have observed that many improvements in auditing standards and techniques are reflected in the pronouncements of the AICPA (generally through the Auditing Standards Board) some time after such improvements are made in the practices of individual firms. More specifically, the pattern seems to be: 1) a problem arises; 2) individual firms conduct research, reach solutions, and implement improvements; 3) the problem is recognized as an issue for study at the Board level; 4) a task force of appropriate practitioners is formed, develops a solution, and submits its recommendations to the Board; and 5) an appropriate pronouncement is issued in due course. Examples of this pattern include: Statement on Auditing Standards (SAS) No. 3 on the effects of EDP on auditing, SAS No. 6 on related-party transactions, and SAS No. 39 on audit sampling.

---

[1]For example, see Bailey and Jensen [1977], Cushing, Searfoss and Randall [1979], Elliott and Rogers [1972], Felix [1974], Kaplan [1973], Kinney [1975a, 1975b], Loebbecke and Zuber [1980], and Turner and Mock [1980]. An excellent review of this literature is provided by Felix and Kinney [1982].

[2]For example, see Bedingfield [1975], Canadian Institute of Chartered Accountants [1980], and Morris and Anderson [1976].

The two major objectives of this study relate to these observations. First, we attempt to develop a better description of the way audits are being done today. We hope that this will serve as a basis for improved understanding of the audit process and its practice and thereby benefit audit researchers in general.

Second, we hope that by providing an analysis of how a number of large firms' audit processes are designed, we can provide a focus on the existing generally accepted auditing standards (GAAS) that may be of service to the Auditing Standards Board in setting its agenda and priorities.

In addition to these major objectives, it is also our objective to provide assistance to researchers and practitioners. We hope to assist researchers in selecting auditing research topics by highlighting areas where underlying research questions exist. We hope to assist practitioners in developing or refining their auditing approaches by developing a general model of the auditing process based on GAAS, and by describing examples of innovative and effective auditing methods presently in use by large accounting firms.

Approach to the Study

To accomplish our objectives, we developed an eight-step approach. The details of these steps are described more fully in later sections.

Step 1—Engage Participants

During the Spring of 1981, we contacted 14 large accounting firms practicing in the United States and invited them to participate in this study. All but two agreed, and we proceeded on the basis of 12 participating firms. They are: Arthur Andersen & Co., Coopers & Lybrand, Deloitte, Haskins & Sells; Ernst & Whinney; Fox & Company; Alexander Grant & Co.; Main Hurdman; Peat, Marwick, Mitchell & Co.; Price Waterhouse; Seidman & Seidman; Touche Ross & Co.; and Arthur Young & Company.

During the summer of 1981, each participating firm furnished us with a copy of materials explaining its audit process in detail. These included general audit manuals, monographs on specialized topics such as auditing in a computer environment, training materials, and copies of forms, questionnaires, and checklists. In addition, each firm designated an individual to serve as a liaison to us in the event we needed assistance in understanding or interpreting the materials provided. In a few cases the materials we received were not complete for our purposes, and we requested and received additional materials from these firms.

Although each of the participating firms was very positive about the objectives of our study and very cooperative with us, they were also understandably sensitive about the confidentiality of their materials, and about inferences concerning their firm that might be drawn from our reported findings. As a condition for obtaining the materials, we agreed to some constraints on the presentation of our findings in order to protect the confidentiality of the data we obtained. Specifically, we are prohibited from associating the name of any of our participating firms with any descriptions of our findings.

Step 2—Develop GAAS Model

Next, we developed a normative model of the audit as a process involving client monitoring, engagement planning, audit testing, opinion formulation, and other activities. This model of the audit process stemmed primarily from a detailed analysis of the Statements on Auditing Standards. The GAAS model developed from this analysis was provided to representatives of the AICPA and of each participating firm. Minor adjustments to this model were made based upon the feedback so obtained. The resulting model is presented in Chapter 2.

Step 3—Develop Individual Firm Models

As each firm's material was received, it was reviewed in detail. Based on this review, we developed a model of the firm's audit process, consisting of a flowchart describing the logical sequence of steps in the process and a narrative description of each step.

Step 4—Compare Individual Firm Models to GAAS Model

Next, we performed a comparative analysis of each individual firm model and the GAAS model. The firm model and this comparison were sent to the firms for their review and comment. This resulted in a dialogue and receipt of additional materials, which enabled us to make appropriate corrections to the initial firm models where necessary.

Step 5—Develop a Cross-Firm Comparison

Once the individual firm models were developed in their final form and compared to the normative GAAS model, it was then possible to make comparisons across all 12 firms and to analyze their similarities and differences. The results of this step are presented in Chapter 3.

Step 6—Analyze Structure

As we proceeded through steps 3 and 4 of the study, an unanticipated dimension became apparent to us. Many firms have consciously developed a systematic approach to their audit process that includes a detailed description of the conceptual logic of the process and a set of audit tools providing detailed guidance to the auditor in carrying out specific audit steps. We refer to this as *structure*. We felt this to be such an important dimension that we extended the cross-firm comparison to provide a comparative analysis of the structure aspects of the firms' methodologies. This is presented in Chapter 4.

Step 7—Identify the Decisions Required in Developing an Audit Methodology

At the conclusion of our study of thousands of pages of materials, we realized that it was possible to identify a pattern of specific decisions that a firm must make in order to establish an audit methodology. We documented this and present it as Appendix B to the study.

Step 8—Develop Conclusions and Recommendation

The conclusions of our study are in the form of a series of overall recommendations based on the broader implications of our study, and a series of detailed recommendations based on our specific observations on the audit methodologies of the participating firms. These are presented in Chapter 5.

Limitations of the Study

An inherent limitation of our approach is that it was restricted to materials published and submitted by the firms for our analysis. There may be additional similarities and differences among the firms that are not apparent from the materials we examined. Such similarities and differences could be revealed by examining firm working papers and by observing how the written policies and procedures are applied in practice. These steps were outside the scope of our study, but represent a potentially worthwhile extension of our research effort.

Another limitation of our approach is that our sample of firms is not representative of all accounting firms. We deliberately chose to include only a limited number of large accounting firms in our study for two reasons: 1) because of a need to limit the volume of materials to be examined to a manageable level, and 2) because of our belief that the auditing approaches of these firms are the most innovative and advanced. However, it is possible that there are additional innovative and advanced auditing approaches and techniques in use by firms not in our sample which we were unable to identify. Exploring this possibility represents another potential extension of this study.

A third limitation of our approach is that our analyses and conclusions are based on published descriptions of firm audit methodologies as of a specific point in time.[3] One thing which has become very clear to us is that all of the firms participating in this study are continuously evaluating, modifying, and extending their auditing methodologies. Accordingly, our conclusions only apply to the auditing approaches of our participating firms as they were described in firm publications at the time of our study. This limitation also applies to our analysis of GAAS, which is based on published standards as of December 31, 1981 (with certain specific exceptions regarding SAS 39 and SAS 43 as explained later in this study).

Another limitation of this study is that its findings and conclusions are based on analyses and interpretations made by the two authors. Given the same data source, other researchers may have performed different analyses, made different interpretations, and perhaps reached different conclusions. The exploratory nature of this study precluded the use of a tight experimental design which might have eliminated potential bias of this kind. This potential problem was exacerbated by the difficulty we faced in attempting to summarize accurately the enormous volume of materials that we received from the firms. We attempted to minimize the effects of this problem by two methods of cross-validation. First, each of us reviewed in less detail the work of the other. Second, intermediate analyses and summaries of our work were reviewed by assigned persons within each firm. Where questions or disagreements arose, additional investigations were performed until a resolution was reached to achieve agreement by all parties.

---

[3]The materials were received from the firms during 1981. Our analysis of the materials was followed by the receipt of feedback from firm representatives pertaining to our analysis, accompanied in some cases by additional firm materials. This process took place over a period of approximately 18 months, concluding in the spring of 1983.

CHAPTER TWO

Analysis of Generally Accepted Auditing Standards

This chapter presents the results of a structured analysis of Statements on Auditing Standards 1 through 39, Statement on Quality Control Standards 1, and an exposure draft of an omnibus SAS (subsequently published as SAS 43).[1] The purpose of this analysis is to construct a formal *model of the audit process* from authoritative literature. This model is used in Chapter 3 as a standard of comparison for the audit methodologies of the 12 participating firms. The analysis in this section is supported by Appendix A: Detailed GAAS References in Support of Audit Process Model, which should be referred to for a more comprehensive explication of each process step.

In performing this analysis, our first step was to prepare a comprehensive outline of the audit process in order to provide a framework for classifying both the material in the Statements on Auditing Standards and the material obtained from the 12 participating firms. This outline is based upon our knowledge and experience with respect to the auditing process, and upon the auditing literature with which we were familiar.[2] The outline identifies the steps in the auditing process in approximately the order they would normally be performed, and classifies the steps into six major categories of activities. The outline appears in Figure 2.1.

As shown in Figure 2.1, the first five major categories of activities which we identify are 1) pre-engagement activities, 2) planning activities, 3) compliance testing activities, 4) substantive testing activities, and 5) opinion formulation and reporting activities. In a typical audit, these activities are performed in approximately this sequence. Our sixth major category—continuous activities—includes those steps which may be performed during any of several stages of an audit and which therefore were not capable of being classified into any of the five sequential categories of activities.

The second step in our analysis was to prepare a flowchart showing in greater detail the logical sequence of the steps contained in our outline. This appears in Figure 2.2. The flowchart is keyed to the outline by means of the reference numbers to the left of each flowchart symbol. The flowchart is divided into five major sections, each corresponding to one of the five major sequential categories of activities in the outline.

Upon completion of the outline and flowchart, we next performed a detailed and comprehensive analysis of the published auditing standards. Each of us independently read the standards and identified any and all references to prescribed auditing procedures or process steps. For each such reference, we noted the step or steps in our outline to which the reference related. Still working independently, we each prepared a list of all of the GAAS references, rearranged according to the sequence of our outline. We then compared our independently prepared lists, discussed their differences in considerable detail, reconciled these differences, and prepared a synthesized list which in our judgment contains the most critical GAAS references relating to each audit process step. This list includes a total of 191 references from the standards, and is contained in Appendix A.

---

[1]SAS 43 was included in the study, in advance of its final publication, because it contains a significant revision to Section 320 of SAS 1 concerning the study and evaluation of internal accounting control, a major element of the audit process.

[2]For example, conceptual models of the auditing process appear in Arens and Loebbecke [1984], Felix and Kinney [1982], Kinney [1975b], and Robertson [1979].

FIGURE 2.1
Comprehensive Outline of the Audit Process

1.0 PRE-ENGAGEMENT ACTIVITIES
- 1.1 Accept/Reject New Client
- 1.2 Establish Terms of Engagement
- 1.3 Assignment of Staff

2.0 PLANNING ACTIVITIES
- 2.1 Obtain Knowledge of the Business
  - 2.11 Preliminary Analytical Review
  - 2.12 Appraisal of Risk
- 2.2 Preliminary Estimation of Materiality
- 2.3 Review of Internal Accounting Control
  - 2.31 Preliminary Phase
  - 2.32 Completion Phase
- 2.4 Develop Overall Audit Plan
  - 2.41 Determine Optimal Reliance on Internal Accounting Control
  - 2.42 Design Compliance Testing Procedures
  - 2.43 Design Substantive Procedures
  - 2.44 Write Audit Program

3.0 COMPLIANCE TESTING ACTIVITIES
- 3.1 Conduct Tests
- 3.2 Make Final Evaluation of Internal Accounting Control
  - 3.21 Make Evaluation
  - 3.22 Modify Audit Plan

4.0 SUBSTANTIVE TESTING ACTIVITIES
- 4.1 Conduct Substantive Tests of Transactions
- 4.2 Conduct Analytical Review Procedures
- 4.3 Conduct Tests of Details of Balances
- 4.4 Post Balance Sheet Review Procedures
- 4.5 Evaluate Results of Substantive Procedures
  - 4.51 Aggregate Findings
  - 4.52 Make Evaluation
  - 4.53 Modify Audit Plan
- 4.6 Obtain Representations
  - 4.61 Management
  - 4.62 Attorneys
  - 4.63 Others

5.0 OPINION FORMULATION AND REPORTING ACTIVITIES
- 5.1 Review Financial Statements
- 5.2 Review Audit Results
- 5.3 Formulate Opinion
- 5.4 Draft and Issue Report

6.0 CONTINUOUS ACTIVITIES
- 6.1 Supervise Conduct of Examination
- 6.2 Review Work of Assistants
- 6.3 Consider Appropriateness of Continuing Relationship with Client

- 6.4 Make Required Special Communications
  - 6.41 Material Weaknesses in Internal Accounting Control
  - 6.42 Material Errors or Irregularities
  - 6.43 Illegal Acts by Client
- 6.5 Consult With Appropriate Persons in Connection With Special Problems
- 6.6 Document Work Performed, Findings, and Conclusions in Appropriate Working Papers

FIGURE 2.2
Flowchart of the Audit Process

KEY:
□ — Step in process, included in GAAS analysis
⬚ — Step in process, not included in GAAS analysis
◇ — Decision or conclusion step

PRE-ENGAGEMENT
ACTIVITIES (1.0)

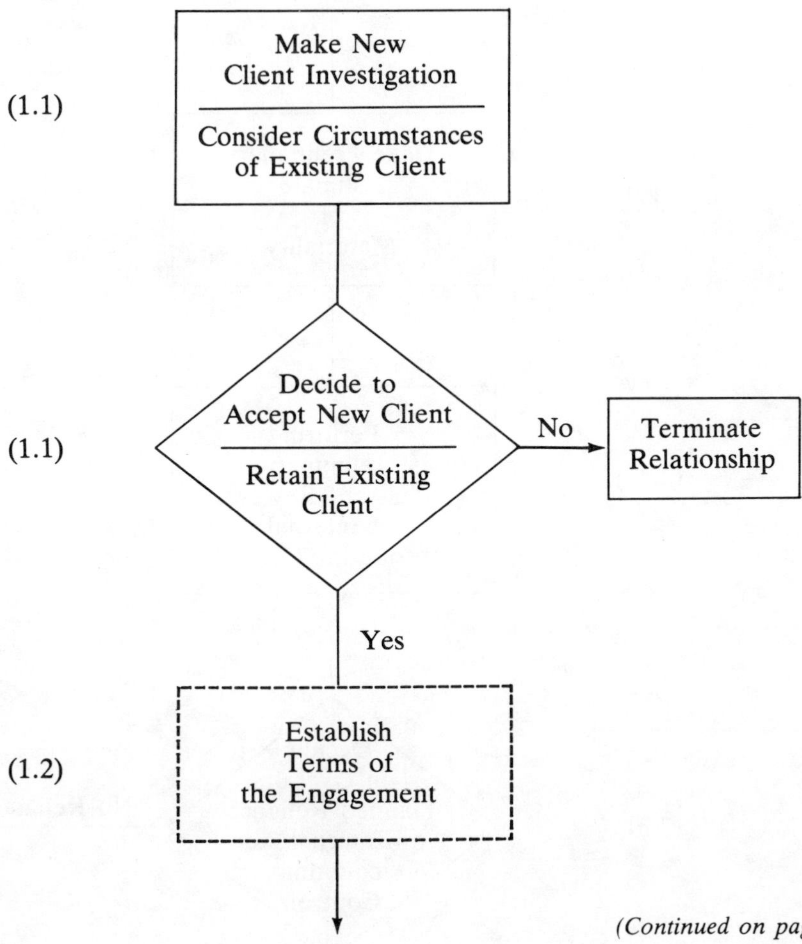

(Continued on page 8)

Figure 2.2 (Continued)

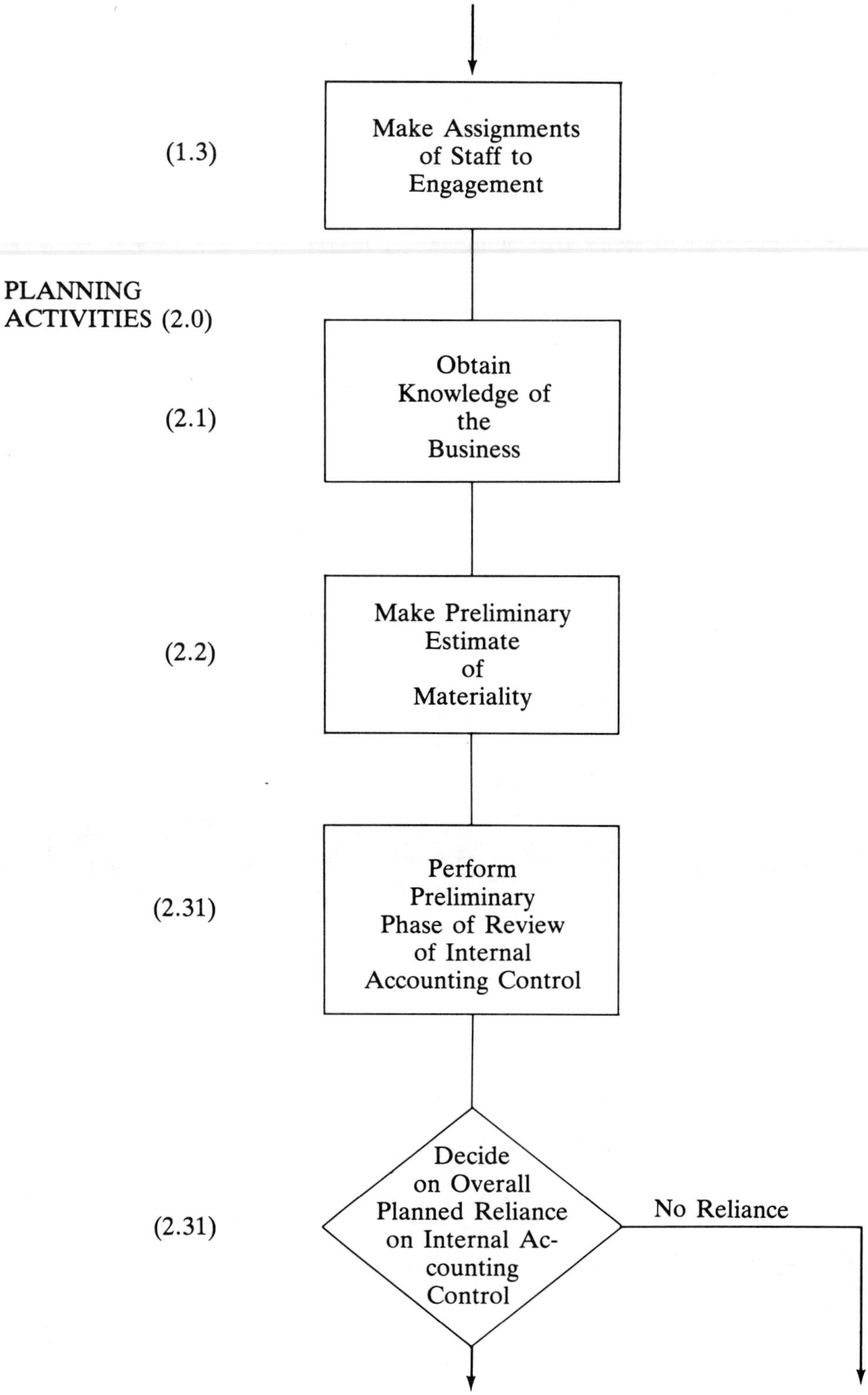

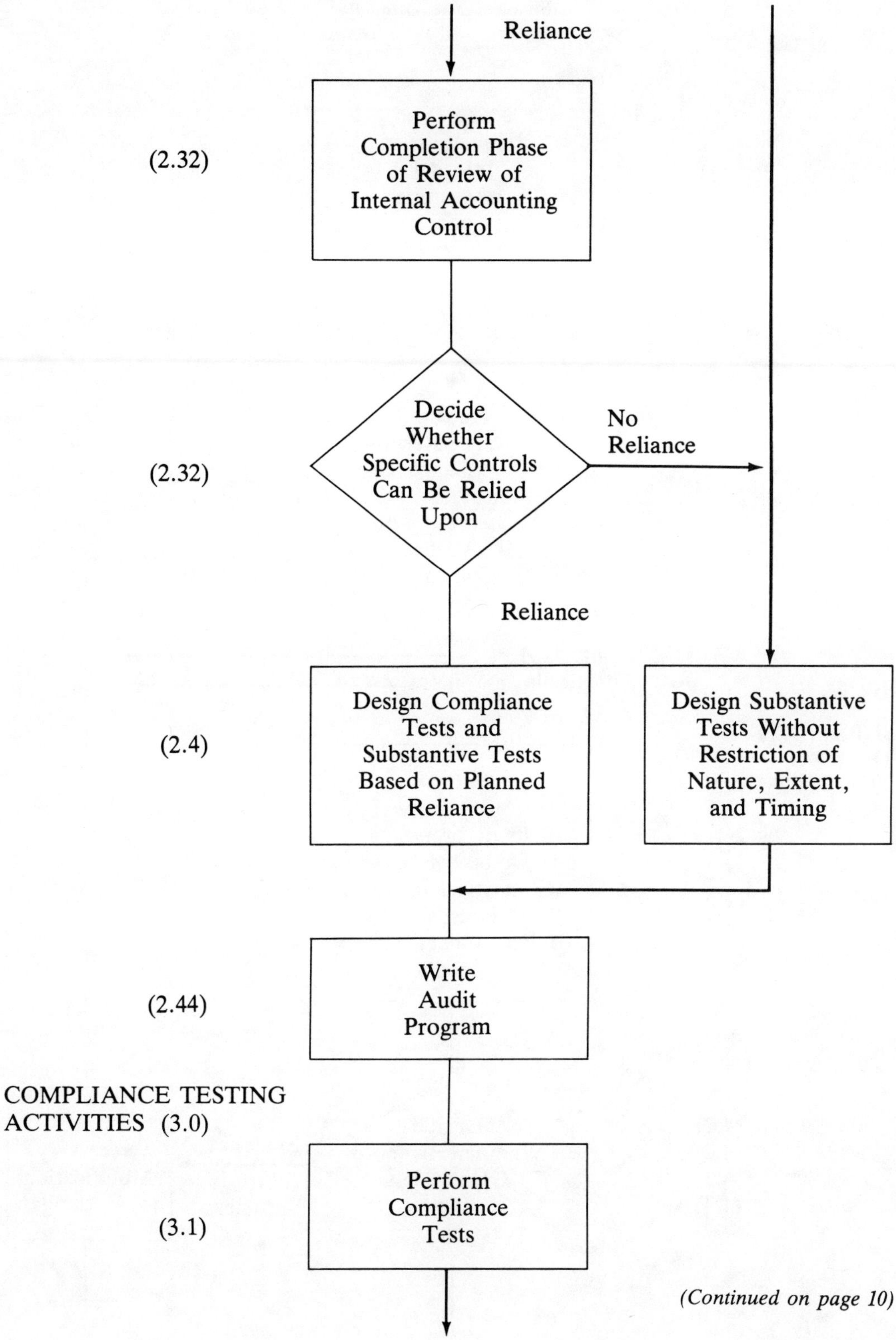

(Continued on page 10)

Figure 2.2 (Continued)

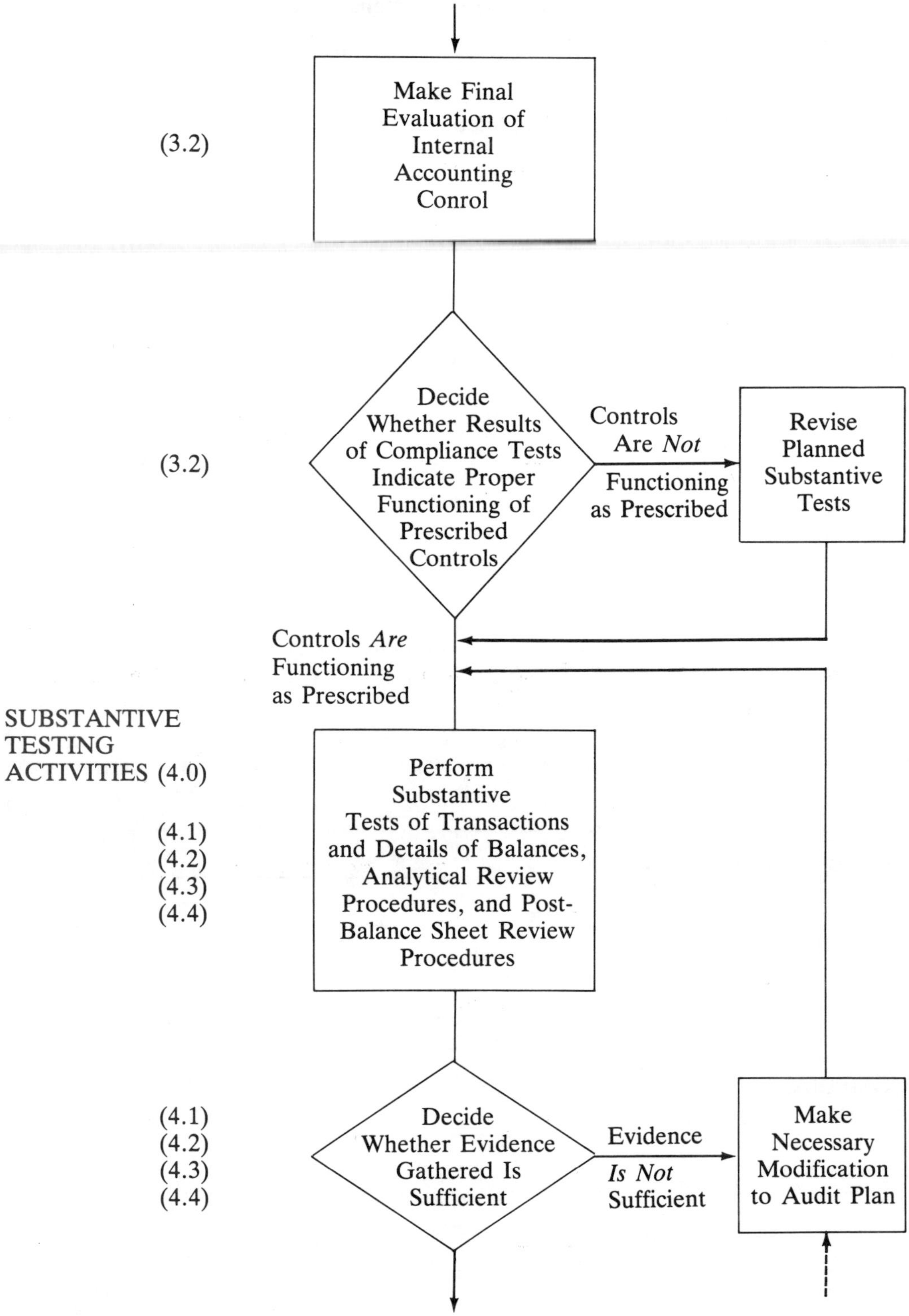

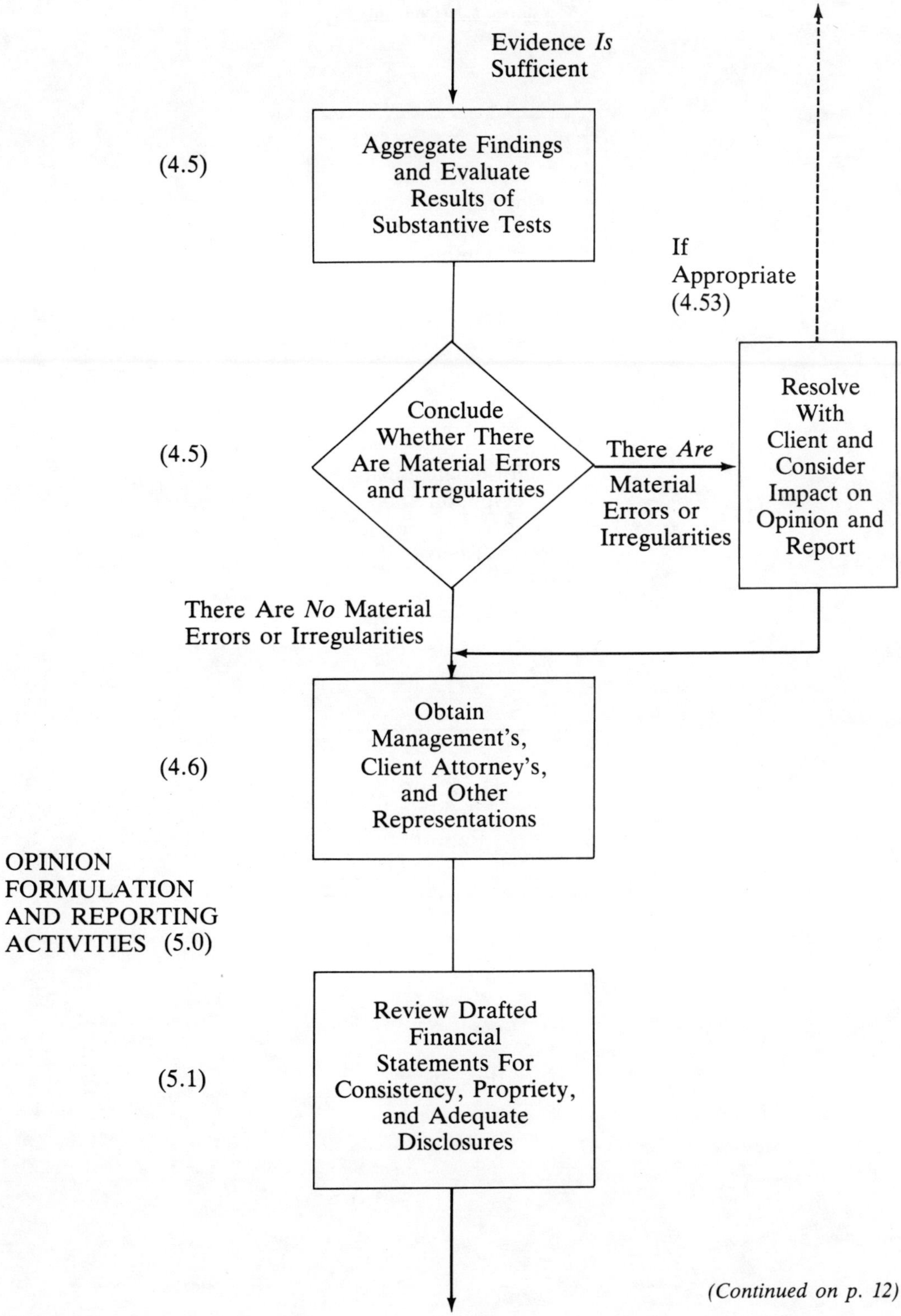

(Continued on p. 12)

Figure 2.2 (Continued)

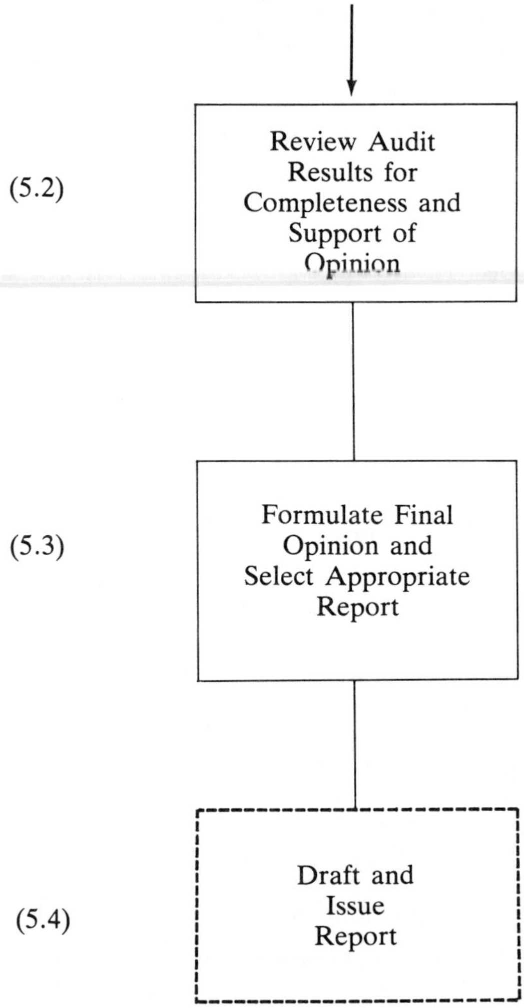

While performing this step, we observed that the codified Statements on Auditing Standards have been arranged in a topical format that does not follow the sequence of activities performed in an audit (as represented by our outline). The framework for organizing the SASs is provided by the ten generally accepted auditing standards. Using this framework, the following major categories of standards may be delineated:

Sections 100-200: General Standards
300: Field Work Standards
300-318: Planning
320-328: Internal Control
330-350: Evidence/Substantive Procedures
400-500: Reporting

To provide an indication of the extent of divergence of the SAS format from the usual sequence of performance of audit activities, we prepared a matrix in which our 191 GAAS references are classified according to the five major SAS categories listed above and according to the six major categories of audit steps included in our outline of the audit process. This matrix appears in Figure 2.3. Each entry in the matrix represents a count of the number of references from the corresponding major SAS category which we included in our corresponding audit process category. References from Statement on Quality Control Standards 1 are included within the General SAS Standards.

The matrix clearly suggests a lack of correspondence between the SAS format and the typical sequence of audit steps. The clearest indication of this is that there are references to audit planning in all of the major sections of the SASs. On reflection, this is not surprising, since each SAS tends to include a discussion of how the issue it deals with should be addressed during audit planning. However, from the perspective of an auditor engaged in audit planning who wishes to examine the relevant standards relating to this task, the fact that such standards are widely scattered throughout the SASs may pose a problem. Furthermore, this problem is not limited solely to planning activities; references to

FIGURE 2.3
Analysis of the GAAS References According to the Audit Process Outline

	SAS Category				
Audit Process Outline Category	General Standards	Planning Standards	Internal Control Standards	Evidence Standards	Reporting Standards
1.0 Pre-engagement	3	1	0	0	0
2.0 Planning	2	22	50	28	4
3.0 Compliance testing	0	0	3	3	0
4.0 Substantive testing	0	3	1	15	3
5.0 Opinion formulation and reporting	3	4	4	15	8
6.C Continuous activities	3	4	10	2	0

opinion formulation and reporting activities may be found in all five major sections of SAS, and references to substantive testing activities may be found in four of the five major sections.

Based on this finding, it may be worthwhile to consider a reorganization of the codified SASs which presents them in a format more consistent with the typical sequence of audit activities. The objective of such a reorganization would be to make the SASs more accessible and useful as a reference tool. This question is addressed in greater detail as part of our recommendations presented in Chapter 5.

CHAPTER THREE
Analysis of Firm Methodologies in Terms of GAAS

Introduction and Comments on Research Approach

In this chapter we summarize the results of a comparison of individual firm audit methodologies with the normative model of the audit process derived by implication from GAAS. We achieve this comparison by the following steps.

For Each Firm

1. A search of each firm's audit process materials was performed to identify audit-process-related contents.
2. A model of the firm's audit process was constructed from these materials.
3. The firm model was compared to the GAAS model to identify:
   a. areas of agreement;
   b. instances where it appeared the firm's material did not include or conform to GAAS requirements; and
   c. instances where it appeared the firm's requirements conformed to but exceeded GAAS requirements.
4. The analysis was reviewed with an appropriate representative of each firm to obtain agreement. In some cases this required modifications of the analyses, which were supported by additional materials provided by the firms.

For All Firms as a Group

5. The information was summarized across all 12 firms.
6. The summary was reviewed by the firms for agreement and approval.

It is important for researchers to understand certain difficulties encountered in the above-described approach. First, the participating firms, although extremely positive about the study as well as cooperative, are very sensitive about the confidentiality of their materials and inferences that might be drawn from our report. This constrains the presentation of results. It certainly would be useful to researchers to see details about each firm's audit process; however, only aggregate data can be shown.

Second, there is the problem of a great amount of data in a nonstandard format. Several of the firms' materials each comprised over 1,000 pages. The format, organizational style, and content varied significantly from firm to firm. Thus, dealing with the data and achieving a complete, accurate, consistent, and objective analysis is difficult. We attempted to deal with this problem by several means:

1. Analyzing each firm's process in two ways:
   a. by constructing a flowchart describing the logical sequence of steps in the process;
   b. by comparing the process to the normative GAAS model;
2. Reviewing the results within the research team; and
3. Reviewing the results with representatives of each firm.

The remainder of this chapter presents a summary of the firms' audit methodologies. This is done for each of the six major segments of the audit as described by the GAAS model:

1. Pre-engagement activities
2. Planning activities
3. Compliance testing activities
4. Substantive testing activities
5. Opinion/reporting activities
6. Continuous activities

For each of these segments, a summary is given for each of the detailed process steps within that segment showing, for the 12 participating firms, the number of firms where:

1. No apparent differences (NAD) with the GAAS model exist;
2. Instances of nonconformity (NC) with the GAAS model exist;
3. Instances where the firm's requirements go beyond GAAS (BG) exist;
4. Other information (O) of relevance and/or interest exists.

(The NAD, NC and BG categories are mutually exclusive; i.e., will add up to 12. The O column is not mutually exclusive of the others.)

Following this summary, there is a descriptive discussion of the findings supporting the NC, BG, and O classifications. It is important to properly interpret the term "nonconformity" (NC) in the context of this classification scheme. NC means that the materials we examined either did not include a specific item that appears in the GAAS literature, or treated a matter in a different way than described in the literature. It should not be inferred from this classification that a firm's audit methods are inadequate, or that the firm is in violation of generally accepted auditing standards. All 12 firms hold their auditors responsible for complying with GAAS as a general policy. Therefore, it can be presumed that items omitted from policy materials are nonetheless performed in the field.

1.0 Pre-Engagement Activities

Summary of findings:

Step	NAD	NC	BG	O
1.1 Accept/reject new clients	11	—	1	1
1.2 Establish terms of engagement	—	—	12	—
1.3 Assignment of staff	8	—	4	5

Step 1.1—Accept/Reject New Client

One firm includes in its accept/reject procedures steps to determine formally the independence of its staff from the prospective client. We know that all large firms have independence review procedures, but they are not intertwined into the audit process to the extent done by this one firm.

A second firm has a requirement to investigate the legal counsel and underwriter of prospective clients proposing public financing. This appears to be a specific extension beyond GAAS, and also beyond the requirements of most other firms.

Step 1.2—Establish Terms of Engagement

All 12 firms require an engagement letter for audit engagements; this is beyond GAAS because there is no such requirement in GAAS. The specific requirements fall into several general groups:

1. A letter is required every year for every engagement, unless approval is obtained for the exception.
2. A letter is obtained on a regular, periodic basis other than annually (e.g., every third year).
3. A letter is obtained in the initial year, and then in subsequent years if conditions or terms change.

Some firms require the client to acknowledge the terms of the engagement by signing and returning a copy of the letter.

Step 1.3—Assignment of Staff

The firms that go beyond GAAS do so by providing requirements for the assignment of a number of specific positions on the audit, and in one case, even responsibilities by audit area. Positions assigned include: engagement partner, manager, tax partner, tax manager, second partner, EDP specialists, statistical specialist, industry specialist, and MAS partner.

In the "other" category:

- Two firms approach the timing of staff assignments in a somewhat different manner than GAAS. That is, they recognize that the need for certain staff unfolds as the engagement progresses, and not all assignments are made at the outset.
- One firm's materials contain an insightful discussion of the audit team concept.
- One firm has a policy that allows managers to have the top responsibility for nonpublic entities rather than always requiring that a partner be assigned to the engagement.
- One firm discusses the use of paraprofessionals in its practice.

2.0 Planning Activities

Summary of findings:

	Steps	NAD	NC	BG	O
2.0	Planning (general)	10	—	2	4
2.1	Obtain knowledge of the business	12	—	—	3
2.11	Preliminary analytical review	8	—	4	—
2.12	Appraisal of risk	8	2	2	2
2.2	Preliminary estimation of materiality	7	5	—	3
2.3	Review of internal accounting control }				
2.31	Preliminary phase }	2	2	8	9
2.32	Completion phase }				
2.4	Develop overall audit plan	7	5	—	4
2.41	Determine appropriate reliance on internal control	12	—	—	—
2.42	Design compliance testing procedures	4	*	8	4
2.43	Design substantive procedures	9	—	3	4
2.44	Write audit program	11	—	1	2

*Several firms have practices in this area which they would argue are in conformity with GAAS, but others might argue the opposite. The details are discussed in that subsection.

Step 2.0—Planning (General)

All 12 firms emphasize the importance of formal planning. However, two firms have specific requirements which caused us to classify them in the "Beyond GAAS" category. The first emphasizes the need to maintain an attitude of "healthy skepticism" on the engagement, and then defines operational criteria used to signal the need for increased skepticism on a particular engagement, with specific reference to challenging management representations.

The second firm requires that planning be documented in an extensive "planning memorandum," which must be signed by the audit partner before any significant audit work can begin.

Two firms use structured, preprinted documents to control the planning process. One firm discusses planning in terms of "strategic planning" for the audit. And finally, one firm has a comprehensive discussion of planning audits of small companies. These are defined as being closely-held, having few administrative personnel, and audit hours of approximately 250 or fewer.

Step 2.1—Obtain Knowledge of the Business

All 12 firms require their auditors to acquire an adequate knowledge of the business as an important planning step. Three firms have other items of interest in this area; one firm includes preparing an inventory of "key variables"—those things that the firm knows about the client that might affect audit scope. A second firm includes a well-defined evaluation of specific "environmental factors." These are categorized as external factors (i.e., industry conditions, regulatory requirements, reporting obligations) and internal factors (i.e., ownership influences, management characteristics, financial characteristics, operating characteristics). A third firm emphasizes that knowledge of the business is cumulative and focuses on building this knowledge base over time.

Step 2.11—Preliminary Analytical Review

All participating firms either conform in kind with this step or appear to have requirements which carry them beyond GAAS. One firm performs preliminary analytical review at two points during planning: first during initial planning, usually in the second or third quarter, and again during the third quarter on a more detailed basis to assist in planning the scope in specific areas.

GAAS makes analytical review during planning an optional step. Three firms make it mandatory, relative to the latest financial statements available during the planning phase.

Step 2.12—Appraisal of Risk

For this step, two firms' materials fail to conform completely with GAAS, two firms go beyond GAAS requirements, and other useful information is provided by two firms.

The two instances of nonconformity are, we suspect, a matter of form rather than substance. Both cases involve a failure to discuss the standards regarding related-party transactions—and in one case, procedures relating to predecessor auditors—to the extent we would expect. This does not mean these procedures are not performed or that the firms disagree with them; only that coverage in the materials we examined is limited.

As to the firms that go beyond GAAS, one uses a structured form to control the appraisal process and presents an interesting discussion of client tax avoidance as a risk consideration. A second firm defines a series of transactions which are of concern. Some of these are relevant to recent SEC and IRS pronouncements. One of the eight firms that does not depart from GAAS requirements implements them through use of a structured form which then is related to later planning decisions.

The two firms in the other category have special forms for the purpose of identifying special engagement risks.

Step 2.2—Preliminary Estimation of Materiality

AU 311.03 requires that during planning, the auditor should establish preliminary estimates of materiality levels (although these need not be specified in quantitative terms). As detailed in the GAAS model, these estimates will be used in several aspects of planning. It is of particular significance, then, to note that five of the 12 firms do not have this requirement. Their materials discuss materiality as a concept in a general or even indirect manner, but specific estimates (either quantified or subjective) appear to be completely avoided. Of all the steps in the GAAS model, there is the greatest degree of nonconformity with this requirement.

Three of the seven firms that do conform provide other useful information. All three of these firms provide extensive, well-written conceptual discussions of materiality. Two of the firms also provide a specific analytical approach for determining amounts and incorporating them into the later steps of their audit process.

Step 2.3—Review of Internal Accounting Control (Including 2.31—Preliminary Phase and 2.32—Completion Phase)

Although there is general (although not complete) conformity with the GAAS model in this area, it is the area, along with accompanying compliance testing, in which the greatest diversity among the firms exists. This is reflected in the number of firms classified in the beyond GAAS and other categories. To understand these differences, some additional analysis is necessary. This is presented below after the instances of nonconformity are described.

Instances of nonconformity. GAAS requires that an evaluation of the control environment and a basic understanding of the flow of transactions be achieved where no reliance is placed on internal control in designing the audit. One firm's materials imply that where no reliance is placed on internal control, perhaps less work than this minimum requirement might suffice. However, the firm's materials are not really definitive on this point and they also indicate that reliance on internal control does exist in varying degrees in most, if not all, audits.

The second instance of nonconformity is the failure of one firm to include a discussion of reliance on internal audit in its materials.

Analysis of differences among firms and other unique features. In this section, an analysis of the 12 firms is presented in terms of eight aspects of the review and evaluation of internal control:

1. Philosophy with regard to reliance
2. Other matters related to philosophy
3. Firm internal control-related tools
4. Extent of work required in the preliminary phase
5. Organization of the study of internal control
6. Use of the transaction walk-through technique
7. Method of expressing results of the study of internal control
8. Method of relating the results of the study to the design of substantive procedures

Each of these is discussed in turn.

1. *Philosophy with regard to reliance.* Where internal control is good, the auditor has a choice between relying or not relying on controls. The firms appear to fall into two groups as to their philosophy about the reliance decision: the materials of the firms in the first group (four firms) are consistent with the GAAS model in the sense that the reliance decision is clearly a matter of auditor discretion; i.e., the policies and/or materials of the firms do not influence the degree of reliance planned. However, in the second group (eight firms), either direct statements or the structure of the process and required materials provide a bias toward reliance on internal control to the extent possible in most audits. (For example, a firm's policy may require the preparation of a detailed internal accounting control questionnaire on every audit engagement.) The general exception would be that on small audits a reliance approach may not be recommended for reasons of economics.
2. *Other matters related to philosophy.* In discussing reliance on internal control, three firms have developed their own unique control theory. These include extensive discussions and the use of unique terms. The auditor is led to discriminate between the types of controls described in terms of both reliance and design of tests.

   Another firm distinguishes itself from the group with an extensive discussion of, and emphasis on, how errors and irregularities could be concealed in connection with their evaluation of internal control. Also, one of the firms includes review of operational controls in its regular audit methodology as an extension of service.
3. *Firm internal control-related tools.* The three major types of internal control-related tools are preprinted questionnaires and checklists, flowcharting systems, and control evaluation matrices. Following is a tabular summary of the use of these tools:
   a. Use of preprinted questionnaires and checklists:

i. Number of firms having extensive preprinted questionnaires and checklists relative to controls	6
ii. Number of firms having guides and criteria in lieu of questionnaires and checklists	5
iii. Number of firms not having significant aids for evaluating system	1
	12

   b. Use of flowcharting:

i. Number of firms that require use of flowcharting	2
ii. Number of firms that encourage use of flowcharting	6
iii. Number of firms that allow use of flowcharting, but take no firm position	3
iv. Number of firms that imply non-use because of other required tools	1
	12

   c. Three firms require the use of a specially constructed matrix which relates control findings to their potential impact on the financial statement accounts.
   d. Table 3.1 shows the combined use by the firms of the above tools.

From this table it appears that flowcharting is considered a useful tool even where questionnaires and preprinted documents are used, but where the latter are not used, an additional evaluation tool (i.e., the matrix) becomes useful.

TABLE 3.1
Use of Certain Tools by Firms

Use of Preprinted Questionnaires and Checklists	Use of Flowcharting	Use of Matrix	No. of Firms
Extensive	Encouraged	Not used	4
Extensive	Allowed	Not used	1
Extensive	Not used	Not used	1
Guides/criteria only	Required	Used	1
Guides/criteria only	Encouraged	Used	1
Guides/criteria only	Encouraged	Not used	1
Guides/criteria only	Allowed	Used	1
Guides/criteria only	Allowed	Not used	1
Not used	Required	Not used	1

4. *Extent of work required in the preliminary phase.* There is a great deal of variation in the amount of documentation, analysis, and evaluation that is required when internal control is not relied on.[1] Six firms require essentially as much documentation, and in some cases evaluation, as where controls are relied upon. Of the remaining six firms, two require an evaluation of controls relative to completeness in all cases, and four require only a review of the control environment and an understanding of the flow of transactions (essentially consistent with SAS 43).
5. *Organization of the study of detailed controls.* All 12 firms refer to making the analysis of controls in terms of transaction cycles (or a similar term). Nine of the firms pre-specify what these cycles should be. Table 3.2 shows (a) the cycles specified and with what frequency, and (b) the number of cycles specified and with what frequency.
   The firms that have a large number of cycles specified achieve this by subdividing some of the cycles shown; for example, by subdividing the revenue cycle into sales and cash receipts.
6. *Use of the transaction walk-through technique.* The SAS states that auditors may trace one or a few transactions through the system to clarify their understanding and description of the system. This is known as a transaction walk-through. The 12 firms vary somewhat in their use of this technique. Four firms require a walk-through of all major accounting systems in all cases. Two firms require a walk-through but only of systems that contain controls being relied upon. Three firms do not require walk-throughs but suggest that they be conducted at the auditor's discretion. Finally, three firms make no mention of the walk-through in their materials at all.

[1]Our study was done during the time SAS 43 was in process. The SAS has since been issued and firm policies may change. Several firms now go beyond GAAS by requiring documentation of the control system when controls are not relied on.

Table 3.2
Cycles Specified

a. Frequency of cycles specified:

Cycle Name (or similar term)	No. of Firms
Revenue cycle (sales-receipts-receivables)	9
Expenditure cycle (purchases-payments-payables)	9
Conversion cycle (production-inventory-cost of sales)	9
Books-records-reporting cycle	7
Payroll cycle	5
Financing cycle	4
Cash-securities (treasury cycle)	3
Property, plant, and equipment	3
Asset accountability	1
Other (catchall)	4

b. Frequency of number of cycles specified:

Number of Cycles	No. of Firms
4	2
5	1
6	2
7	1
8	1
9	1
12	1
	9

7. *Method of expressing results of the study of internal control.* There appear to be two general approaches to expressing the results of the study of internal control. The first approach—which might be termed the comprehensive approach—is to make and express a judgment on every pertinent control objective. This is done by seven firms with some variation in the mode of expression; i.e., some are done in terms of objectives (two firms), some in terms of risks (two firms), and some in terms of the likelihood of errors (three firms).

   The remaining five firms use what might be termed the exception approach. These firms express the results in terms of the identification of weaknesses in internal control, and the impact of those weaknesses.
8. *Method of relating the results of the study to the design of substantive procedures.* Six of the 12 firms have a very detailed, structured approach to establishing this relationship. One of the six firms accomplishes it through use of extensive preprinted documents, while the other five rely more on guides and criteria, with some use of preprinted documents such as the matrices mentioned under item 3 above. The second group of six firms does not approach this problem at the same level of structure and detail. These firms rely primarily on the auditor's judgment and

thought processes to discern the impact of internal control evaluation results on substantive tests.

An analysis of the relationship between the method of expressing results and the methods of relating results to substantive procedures by firm is as follows:

Method of Relating Results to Substantive Procedures	Method of Expressing Results of Study	
	Comprehensive Approach	Exception Approach
Structured—use of preprinted documents		1
Structured—use of guides and criteria	5	
Not structured—reliance on auditor judgment	2	4

Another dimension to this that does not appear on the above table is that the firms in the largest cell (five) are ones that have recently revised their audit approaches. It would appear to us that when these firms developed their new methods it was natural that they accompanied the extensive discussion of detailed objectives with appropriate guides and criteria. An interesting observation is that they did not choose extensive use of preprinted documents to operationalize their approach. Possible reasons for this are considered in the portion of this study on structure.

Step 2.4—Develop Overall Audit Plan

All 12 firms' methodologies result in an overall audit plan. The form of documentation of the plans varies among the firms. For example, some firms require an extensive memorandum documenting the plan which must contain specific elements of information, others require a detailed form to be prepared, while still others rely on a less structured memorandum, or perhaps a section in the audit program.

GAAS require that preliminary estimates of materiality be integrated into the audit plan, although they need not be specified in quantitative terms. Five firms do not formally require consideration of such estimates, which is inconsistent with the requirements of GAAS. In addition, one of the firms makes no mention in its materials of the need to consider the use of specialists as part of the plan.

Most of the firms give some emphasis to the use of advanced auditing techniques as part of their development of the overall audit plan. These include analytical review, statistical sampling, computer-assisted audit techniques, and reliance on and use of internal audit. It is difficult to classify firms as to their position on these techniques;

however, they all appear to strive for efficiency and to wish to be "progressive" as auditors.

Several firms' materials contain detailed discussion of specific audit planning issues that we found interesting and informative. These are:

- The significance of the sequence in which tests are performed;
- The theory and practice of performing tests at an interim date;
- Ways of achieving efficiency—particularly by using cumulative knowledge and rotation of work between organizational units over time; and
- Extensive guides to specific procedures.

Step 2.41—Determine Appropriate Reliance on Internal Control

As indicated under Step 2.3, eight firms' policies and/or materials appear to influence their auditors toward a reliance approach, except perhaps in the case of audits of small companies. We don't interpret this as a matter of nonconformity with GAAS, as the firms do decide the appropriate reliance and certainly don't rely on controls where such reliance is not justified. However, we observe that this influence might result in auditors taking an approach which is not always the most efficient one. Of course, this is speculative and would require some empirical investigation to substantiate.

Step 2.42—Design Compliance Testing Procedures

The process of reviewing and evaluating internal control ends with the conduct of compliance tests and integration of their results with other internal control information. Although all 12 firms agree that compliance tests are applied to controls being relied upon, there is extensive disagreement on what constitutes a compliance test and how such tests are performed.

What constitutes a compliance test? There are two matters at issue here: reperformance and reliability of observations as a form of evidence. Reperformance involves testing the accounting procedures which created a document by redoing them to establish whether the document contains monetary errors. All firms agree that a test of controls involving the inspection of documents should contain an examination of the visible indications that the control has been applied (e.g., approval signatures). Several firms believe that reperformance must also be included in the test. These firms would argue that the auditor cannot know whether the control actually worked unless he or she determines whether the related transaction is correct or in error.

Several other firms take the opposite position. They would argue that the purpose of compliance tests is to look for compliance evidence, e.g., approval signatures. Although existence of such evidence does not guarantee the absence of errors, this is recognized by the restriction of substantive tests, not their elimination. These firms believe that reperformance is a substantive test—just one of several alternative types—and that it is inappropriate to call it what it is not. They would argue further that reperformance would only tell the auditor if a control worked where he or she knew the transaction was initially in error and was corrected by the control; but this is seldom, if ever, known.

Below is a summary of firm positions on this question.

Position	**No. of Firms**
Reperformance specifically required on all tests of transaction documents relating to controls	3

Reperformance specifically required, but only on certain types of controls	2
Reperformance not specifically required, but accomplished due to extensive use of dual-purpose tests	3
Reperformance not done in testing compliance but specifically identified as a substantive test	4
	12

All 12 firms recognize that compliance tests will include observations as well as tests of documents. At least one firm maintains that the reliability of observations as a form of audit evidence is below that of tests of documents, and their use should be limited. Conversely, at least one firm maintains that the opposite is true.

A further symptom of the disagreement (or perhaps confusion) with respect to compliance tests is the fact that two firms have abandoned, at least partially, the SAS terminology on this subject and have adopted unique terms that they feel are more descriptive of what is actually being done.

How are compliance tests performed? There are two issues relating to this question: timing and sampling methodology. Most of the firms follow the practice of spreading compliance tests over most, if not all, of the audit period using some systematic method. However, there are some exceptions: one firm believes that there are certain types of controls for which it is better not to spread the tests, but to investigate them in depth at a point in time. Four firms spread the tests they conduct over time, but they also cycle some tests over audit years. In other words, they don't test all controls they rely on to the same extent every year. There may be some contention as to whether these practices are consistent with GAAS. We have heard it argued that GAAS specifically requires formal, detailed compliance testing of each specific control being relied upon to the same ("full") extent each year. Firms that either don't spread tests or cycle would argue, by reference to AU 320.60 (AU 320.62 as of June 1985), that "The purpose of compliance tests is to provide reasonable assurance that the accounting control procedures are being applied as prescribed." They would assert that the design of procedures for this purpose is essentially a matter of auditor judgment, and that their methods are both cost-efficient and effective in that context. We have concluded that the position of these firms is acceptable, and have not listed it as an instance of nonconformity, but as an "other" item.

The major issues in the area of sampling policy are whether statistical or non-statistical methods should be used and what sample sizes are appropriate. The following summarizes firm policies with respect to the method used:

Policy	**No. of Firms**
Statistical sampling strongly encouraged or required	5
Statistical sampling preferred	3
Statistical or non-statistical at the auditor's discretion	3
Non-statistical sampling preferred	1
	12

It is difficult to present an analysis of the firms' requirements regarding sample size for compliance tests. Some firms' requirements are specific and some are not; some specify sample size, while others specify statistical parameters to be used to determine sample size. Some vary the requirements with the degree of planned reliance on controls. To provide a rough approximation of sample size policies, we would expect most firms' compliance tests to fall within a range of 25 to 60 items, with adjustment upwards where errors are found.

One firm has an interesting additional requirement for compliance tests. It requires that when key attributes (controls) are tested, the auditor should make inquiries of the responsible individuals to determine that they understand their responsibilities and how exceptions are resolved.

This subsection has described several important auditing issues. We have essentially accepted firm positions on these issues in this paper. However, we have recognized that they are contentious and suggest to policy makers that they are worthy of attention and further resolution.

Step 2.43—Design Substantive Procedures

One matter that we noted in this area that was initially treated as an instance of nonconformity with GAAS was that several firms had not integrated the requirements of SAS 39 into their materials. However, the Auditing Standards Board moved the effective date of SAS 39 to June 25, 1983; thus, we do not treat this as an exception.

Three firms have requirements exceeding GAAS in the design of substantive tests. One firm believes that positive confirmations are far more effective than the negative form and should be considered the norm. A second firm includes required procedures for the formal review and testing of client judgments and nonroutine processes, believing that these represent additional risk. A third firm defines several specific audit objectives that must be accomplished with tests of details to recognize identified risks.

Several firms use an objectives-oriented approach to designing substantive procedures. These are consistent with SAS 31, although unique terminology or grouping of objectives is often used. As was pointed out in discussing Step 2.3, some firms use special tools and analyses to evaluate the impact of systems findings on substantive tests. In describing specific tests, several firms' materials contain a wealth of information and procedures that might be performed.

Two firms make unique contributions to audit technology. One of these is a fairly complete system for determining materiality and its integration into the design of each test. The other is a discussion of the significance of the direction of errors *vis-à-vis* audit tests.

Step 2.44—Write Audit Program

All 12 firms require a written audit program, along with requirements for appropriate review and approval. One firm was classified "beyond GAAS" because its approval requirements are very stringent and do not allow any tests to be performed prior to partner approval.

Two firms provide preprinted programs of substantive tests that are completed by having the auditor add, change, and delete procedures.

3.0 Compliance Testing Activities

Eleven of the firms' materials explicitly conform with the GAAS model in this area, one goes beyond GAAS, and four have aspects placing them in the other category. Steps

2.3 and 2.42 include a discussion of our findings with regard to this section of the audit process, and no further comments are necessary.

4.0 Substantive Testing Activities

Summary of findings:

Step	NAD	NC	BG	O
4.1 Conduct substantive tests of transactions	12	—	—	2
4.2 Conduct analytical review procedures	9	—	3	3
4.3 Conduct tests of details of balances	12	—	—	2
4.4 Post-balance-sheet review procedures	11	1	—	—
4.5 Evaluate results of substantive procedures	12	—	—	2
4.6 Obtain representations	12	—	—	4

Step 4.1—Conduct Substantive Tests of Transactions

AU 320.70 defines substantive tests as comprising analytical review procedures and tests of details of transactions and balances. Substantive tests of transactions may be performed as a separate set of tests or combined with compliance tests that relate to the same underlying documents (i.e., dual-purpose tests). Different firms treat substantive tests of transactions in one or the other of these contexts depending on their philosophy and process. Firms that emphasize reperformance tend to include these tests in the systems phase of the audit as dual-purpose tests or as compliance tests with little substantive evidence emphasis. Other firms will identify these procedures as a separate class and may use them to establish a low rate of monetary errors in a transaction stream even where formal controls do not exist. This, essentially, allows these firms to restrict substantive tests of balances, as where controls are being relied upon.

Step 4.2—Conduct Analytical Review Procedures

GAAS leave to the auditor's discretion the proper mix between substantive tests of details and analytical review procedures. The emphasis given to analytical review in the materials we reviewed leads us to believe that all 12 firms apply some analytical review procedures on all, or at least most, audits. One firm requires analytical review in every audit area as a specific policy. Another firm has a policy which dictates the staff level of the person who must conduct the analytical review (i.e., the senior or manager), and a third firm has a policy that requires the auditor to test the underlying data when analytical revew is an important element in support of an account balance.

One of the firms that uses analytical review procedures extensively has an excellent discussion in its materials. This discussion not only lists useful ratios and procedures, but relates them to specific error types. That firm also has an interesting policy on interpreting analytical results that result in differences between the analysis and the client's recorded book value. If the client's system of internal control is good, differences (unless material) are assumed to be imprecisions in the analysis. However, if the client's system is weak, the differences are assumed to represent errors.

Unique features of other firms' materials include one firm's discussion of the relevance of the timing of analytical review with respect to other tests, and the use by another firm of some very sophisticated, computer-based analytical review techniques.

Step 4.3—Conduct Tests of Details of Balances

It was mentioned in an earlier step that the firms have not yet necessarily incorporated the requirements of SAS 39 into their materials, but that this would not be treated as an exception in this analysis. It is appropriate to point out here that several firms have all the requirements of SAS 39 in their materials and have probably been following them for some time.

The main omission in the cases where the requirements of SAS 39 are absent relates to extending the results of tests of details to the entire population sampled.

Most firms have a significant body of materials on the nature and performance of substantive procedures. The materials of two firms were particularly comprehensive.

Step 4.4—Post-Balance-Sheet Review

There is general conformity with this step in the GAAS model. The one instance of nonconformity is the absence in the firm's materials of the procedures in SAS 34 regarding clients where the going-concern assumption might not apply.

Step 4.5—Evaluate Results of Substantive Procedures

The observation made in Step 4.3 regarding SAS 39 applies equally here. However, there is broad conformity with this step.

The two firms in the other category are so indicated because they have both developed structured, quantitative approaches to combining the results of various tests, including tests of different accounts.

Step 4.6—Obtain Representations

All 12 firms are in conformity with this requirement of GAAS. Several of the firms have special procedures that are of interest:

- One firm makes provision for obtaining representations from specialists and other auditors.
- One firm requires two separate letters: one from the CEO and CFO regarding general matters, and another from the corporate secretary regarding the minutes.
- One firm requires a separate representation letter regarding the proposed journal entries that clients are to accept and record in their books.
- One firm has a comprehensive set of procedures for documenting all informal representations obtained throughout the engagement.

5.0 Opinion Formulation and Reporting Activities

Summary of findings:

Step	NAD	NC	BG	O
5.1 Review financial statements	9	—	3	1
5.2 Review audit results	12	—	—	—
5.3 Formulate opinion	12	—	—	—
5.4 Draft and issue report	—	—	12	—

Step 5.1—Review Financial Statements

The SASs indicate that the auditor may perform analytical review procedures as an overall review of the financial statements. One firm has a specific requirement to do this.

The other two firms whose requirements exceed GAAS have mandatory procedures for determining that the books and records agree with the financial statements to be issued. This was a guideline in AU 338.05a; however, it is stated as a requirement in SAS 41, which was issued after the effective date of our review.

Several firms have financial statement preparation checklists that are very comprehensive.

Step 5.2—Review Audit Results

All 12 firms conform with GAAS, but in effect go beyond it in this area. The firms all have SEC clients and general concerns with quality and controlling risk. Thus, each firm has a review system that has various levels of review. These include an independent, pre-issuance review by a second partner, or in some cases, a review department. Each firm also has some form of post-issuance inspection program, referencing such matters as involvement of specialists.

Certainly, there is adequate review. Our belief, based on this brief analysis, is that 1) there may be excessive review, and 2) the process of review with all of its behavioral aspects is an area deserving of further study.

Step 5.3—Formulate Opinion

All firms conform with this step, as one would expect, and have extensive supporting materials to assist auditors in so doing.

Step 5.4—Draft and Issue Report

Whereas the professional literature does not speak to the practical details and administrative aspects of drafting and issuing the auditor's report, these matters are covered extensively in the firms' materials. These procedures include typing, proofreading, reproduction, distribution, and filing. The firms use control procedures to assure all steps have been followed and, in particular, that distribution of reports is appropriate and authorized.

6.0 Continuous Activities

Summary of findings:

Step	NAD	NC	BG	O
6.1 Supervise conduct of examination	12	—	—	—
6.2 Review work of assistants	12	—	—	—
6.3 Consider appropriateness of continuing relationship with client	12	—	—	4
6.4 Make required special communications	10	1	1	—
6.5 Consult with appropriate persons in connection with special problems	12	—	—	—
6.6 Document work performed, findings, and conclusions in appropriate working papers	12	—	—	—

Steps 6.1, 6.2, and 6.5 all represent areas where the GAAS model is conformed with by all 12 firms and there are no apparent significant differences among the firms. Thus, further discussion of these steps is unnecessary.

Step 6.3—Consider Appropriateness of Continuing Relationship with Client

All firms have this requirement, but some firms' approaches to it are worth noting. Two firms, for instance, have a requirement early in their process to "determine that the entity is auditable before the engagement can proceed." Presumably, conditions which preclude a continuing relationship would surface during this step. Two other firms require specific documentation of the process of considering the relationship and the decision to continue it.

Step 6.4—Make Required Special Communications

One firm's materials have no discussion about communicating with the client regarding material errors and irregularities and illegal acts.

In the beyond GAAS category, one firm also defines and requires communication about "sensitive transactions." The majority of the firms require their special communications to be in writing, although the SAS allows verbal communication.

Step 6.6—Document Work Performed, Findings, and Conclusions in Appropriate Working Papers

All 12 firms have extensive documentation policies and systems. These vary from firm to firm and are integrated into each firm's methodology. Information about documentation requirements has been given under various steps and is discussed further in the section on structure.

Other

In reviewing the firms' materials for conformity with the GAAS model, a number of matters were covered in those materials that are not in GAAS. A listing of these follows.

- Engagement administration including:
  - —The handling of multi-office engagements
  - —Responsibilities and duties of the partner as well as various staff levels
  - —Engagement team meetings
  - —Engagement budgeting procedures
  - —Staff appraisal procedures
  - —Retention of working papers
- The use of other auditors
- Management letters
- Attending annual shareholders' meetings
- Special considerations for audits of small businesses

One firm had a unique technical discussion in its materials that deserves mention. This is a discussion as a separate subject of audit control procedures; i.e., those procedures the auditor must follow to assure that client personnel can't improperly interfere with the auditor's procedures and findings. The materials place particular emphasis on EDP activities.

Summary

In this chapter we reported the extent of explicit coverage in firm policies and procedures of the detailed steps of the GAAS model, as evidenced by the firm materials provided to us. Of course, we have no way of knowing in this study the degree to which actual firm practices conform to these policies; however, we point out that the mission of the profession's peer review program is to investigate that question. We also reported differences among the firms and other matters of interest that we were able to observe. Undoubtedly, further study of the materials, which numbered in the many thousands of pages, would reveal additional matters of interest. Similarly, many of the areas noted by us deserve more detailed analysis and thought. Such is the nature of all research projects: in seeking to answer some questions, they manage to raise many additional ones.

Certainly the most important findings in this section relate to any indication of failure by the firms to conform to GAAS model requirements. This might imply that 1) the requirements are onerous in some way and not acceptable to practitioners, or even 2) that the firms are performing at a level below professional standards. The instances of nonconformity noted fall into the following groups:

- First, there were a number of instances where firms failed to specifically discuss an area of GAAS in the materials we reviewed. This may be viewed as a nonserious problem in the sense that the firms' policies do not contradict GAAS; it's just that firm personnel must rely on references beyond firm materials to know the requirements and to obtain guidance.
- Second, there are instances where firm policies may lack conformity with GAAS depending on how GAAS is interpreted. These occur particularly in the area of compliance testing. Additional research and clarification of standards may be appropriate for these items.
- Third, there is one area of extensive nonconformity: that of considering preliminary estimates of materiality during audit planning. Five firms exclude this requirement from their audit guidance. This would seem to be a requirement that is unacceptable to a major portion of auditor-constituents and thus requires serious reexamination.
- With the possible exception of lack of guidelines for developing materiality estimates during planning, the 12 firms are clearly in conformity with GAAS. In fact, they have many requirements beyond GAAS. This means that the standards are considered to be a floor for performance, not a ceiling.
- Many differences among the firms are noticeable, particularly in terms of their attitude toward the importance of evaluating internal control, the design of compliance tests, and related matters. There also are differences in structure and style that are discussed in the next chapter. The materials of the firms are well-written and contain a wealth of information on auditing. Together, the materials of these 12 firms comprise the most comprehensive set of auditing literature ever assembled.

CHAPTER FOUR

Analysis of Firm Methodologies in Terms of Structure

One difference among the audit approaches of the firms we studied became very apparent as our research progressed. There are significant differences in the degree of structure of audit processes. In this chapter we examine the degree of structure present in the audit approaches of the 12 firms.

We define a *structured audit methodology* as a systematic approach to auditing characterized by a prescribed, logical sequence of procedures, decisions, and documentation steps, and by a comprehensive and integrated set of audit policies and tools designed to assist the auditor in conducting the audit. A structured audit methodology is *systematic* in the sense that it views the auditing process as a logical series of steps, often explicitly represented in the form of an audit process flowchart. The audit policies and tools used in a structured audit methodology are *comprehensive* in the sense that they cover the entire auditing process, from the initial acceptance of the client to the ultimate issuance of the audit opinion. The audit tools are *integrated* by means of a top-down approach to the design of the entire set of audit tools, such that the results from applying one audit tool at an earlier stage of the audit may be incorporated into other audit tools used in planning later stages of the audit.

Our concept of a structured audit methodology bears some resemblance to the concept of the "mechanistic" audit discussed by Dirsmith and McAllister [1982a, 1982b]. They describe the mechanistic audit as characterized by strict definition of organizational goals, the use of highly formalized decision-making processes, extensive documentation, comprehensive review procedures, and the development of highly formalized authority structures. Our concept of a structured audit methodology includes elements of all of these characteristics except the development of highly formalized authority structures. However, our audit structure concept is not inconsistent with the central elements of Dirsmith and McAllister's antithesis of the mechanistic audit, which they refer to as the "organic" audit; these features include emphasis on the individual auditor's judgment and on adapting the audit approach to the unique characteristics of the client, and a loose approach to the exertion of centralized control over organizational members. Specifically, the importance of auditor judgment and of adapting the audit approach to the client organization were stressed in virtually all of the firm materials we examined, regardless of whether or not the firm's audit approach was highly structured. With respect to the degree of exertion of centralized control over field auditors, we can draw no firm conclusions because our analysis was restricted to published firm materials dealing primarily with auditing methods. However, in our view the use of highly structured audit guidance is not necessarily inconsistent with a loose form of centralized control. In conclusion, the concept of the mechanistic audit should not be equated with our description of highly structured audit approaches, because (despite their similarities) there are significant differences between the two concepts.

In this chapter we describe a method that we developed to measure the degree of structure in a firm's audit methodology. We then describe the results of applying this measurement method to the audit processes of our 12 subject firms. From this analysis, several profiles are developed of audit methodologies having various degrees of structure. Next, we describe the motivation for structure and the possible advantages and disadvantages that a firm might realize from a more structured audit methodology. The chapter concludes with a brief discussion of the research implications of the audit structure concept.

Measurement of Audit Structure

The approach that we used to measure audit structure could be described as a gross form of content analysis. Operationally, content analysis requires the identification of "units of analysis" and of "systems of enumeration" for each unit [Holsti, 1968]. Our units of analysis were based upon 18 elements of a firm's audit methodology which we identified as capable of differentiating its degree of structure. These were classified into the following six major categories: (A) the overall audit process, (B) initial audit planning, (C) audit program design, (D) control review and evaluation, (E) use of audit tools, and (F) documentation and review. The complete set of 18 elements of audit structure, broken down into these six categories, appears in Figure 4.1.

For each element of audit methodology, the unit of analysis consisted of the portion of the firm's audit guidance that dealt with that element. Our system of enumeration consisted of the assignment of a score from one (least structured) to five (most structured) to each firm's approach with respect to each of the 18 elements of audit structure. Thus, the maximum structure score that a firm could obtain under this scoring technique is 90 (a score of five on each of the 18 elements), while the minimum possible score is 18.

To ensure consistency of application of our scoring procedure, one of the researchers performed the initial review and assignment of scores for all 12 firms. These assignments were reviewed by the other researcher, and differences were resolved through references to underlying materials and discussion. The ratings were not cross-validated by firm personnel.

Our system of enumeration was based upon the following units of enumeration: 1) the length of the material; 2) a categorization of the types of material, including (a) narrative, (b) checklists, (c) preprinted forms, (d) questionnaires, (e) formulas, (f) computer programs, (g) flowcharts, (h) matrices, and (i) diagnostic techniques; 3) a judgment as to whether the materials were primarily of a qualitative or analytical nature; and 4) an assessment of the degree of integration of the materials dealing with each element of audit structure with the other elements. The distinction between qualitative and analytical guidance was based upon whether the materials concentrated solely on identifying those factors that should be considered by the auditor in forming a particular judgment (qualitative guidance), or whether the materials also provided explicit guidelines for reaching specific conclusions based upon the nature of the evidence relating to particular factors (analytical guidance). The degree of integration of materials was assessed by evaluating the extent to which the results or conclusions obtained from audit procedures associated with one element of audit structure were explicitly used as a basis for planning or executing audit procedures associated with other elements of audit structure.

Once the firm's materials had been reviewed and a judgment reached concerning each of these units of enumeration, a score was assigned for each element of audit structure based upon the following rules. If the element was not dealt with in the firm's materials, or dealt with in only a short passage in narrative form, a score of one was assigned. If the element was dealt with in a section of moderate length in narrative form and with primarily qualitative guidance, a score of two was assigned. If the element was dealt with in a section of moderate length which included nonnarrative types of material and analytical guidance, or was dealt with in a section of extensive length, then a judgment was made concerning the degree of sophistication of the guidance as a whole relating to that particular element of audit structure. If the guidance was judged to be of relatively limited sophistication, a score of three was assigned. If the guidance was judged to be of relatively high sophistication, then an assessment was made of the degee of integration of the materials relating to that element with materials relating to other elements. If the degree of integration was judged to be low, a score of four was assigned; if high, a score of five was assigned. This process was repeated for each of the 18 elements of audit structure to obtain a total structure score for each firm.

FIGURE 4.1
Elements Used in Measurement of Audit Structure

A. Overall audit process

1. General nature and content of audit process
2. Form of description of audit process

B. Initial audit planning

3. Extent of formal planning
4. Staffing requirements and use of specialists
5. Criteria for judgments on risk
6. Criteria for judgments on materiality
7. Planning documentation requirements

C. Audit program design

8. Use of preprinted forms and programs
9. Tradeoff between control reliance and substantive approach
10. Criteria for sample design

D. Control review and evaluation

11. Format for description of systems
12. Use of preprinted questionnaires

E. Use of audit tools

13. Analytical review methods
14. Computer audit tools
15. Statistical sampling methods

F. Documentation and review

16. Documentation requirements
17. Review requirements
18. Standards checklists

We acknowledge the limitations of this scoring procedure. Our selection of the 18 elements of audit structure was entirely subjective. Although our scoring procedure was partially objective, it required many subjective judgments as well. We chose to aggregate the structure scores using a simple sum method, although a weighted sum would have been more appropriate if some elements of audit structure are more important than others. In some cases, it was not clear that we had received a complete set of materials from the firm. In other cases the firm's materials were clearly in a transition stage, and their scores might change substantially if they were based on more current materials. Despite these limitations, we feel that our scoring procedure does identify many significant differences among the firms' approaches which may be characterized as differences in audit structure.

Figure 4.2 summarizes the results obtained from applying our scoring procedure to the 12 subject firms. The firms are ranked from one (most structured) to 12 (least structured), with both the total structure score and average score per element shown. The 12 firms tended to cluster into four well-differentiated categories. The two firms with the most structured audit methodologies have average scores well over four; these are subsequently referred to as the "highly structured" audit methodologies. Next is a group of four firms with audit methodologies clustered tightly around an average score of 3.5; these are subsequently labeled "semistructured" methodologies. The third group consists of four firms whose audit methodologies were assigned scores which averaged approximately 2.8; these methodologies shall henceforth be referred to as "partially structured." The audit methodologies of the remaining two firms received average scores substantially below 2.5, and are subsequently referred to as "unstructured."

Next, an analysis was performed to determine whether the differences in degree of structure among these four categories of audit methodology tended to be concentrated into any of the six categories of audit structure elements delineated in Figure 4.1. This was accomplished by computing the average score for each category of audit methodology within each category of audit structure element. The results are summarized in Figure 4.3. The results display an astonishing consistency among the six categories of audit structure. Within each and every category, the highly structured audit methodologies received substantially higher average scores than those of the semistructured audit methodologies, which in turn were substantially higher than the average scores of the partially structured audit methodologies, which in turn were substantially higher than the average scores of the unstructured audit methodologies. The smallest difference in average scores for any pair of adjacent scores in the table is 0.25. We believe that the consistency of these results

FIGURE 4.2
Structure Scores for Subject Firms

Firm Number and Rank	Total Score	Average Score	Firm Number and Rank	Total Score	Average Score
1	81	4.50	7	53	2.94
2	76	4.22	8	51	2.83
3	66	3.67	9 (tie)	49	2.72
4	64	3.56	9 (tie)	49	2.72
5	62	3.44	11	42	2.33
6	61	3.39	12	39	2.17

provides strong evidence for the validity of our technique for measuring audit structure. At the very least, the measurement technique has clearly and consistently differentiated four distinct categories of audit methodology, as measured along these six dimensions of the audit process.

A more systematic measure of the internal consistency of the structure scores across the 18 elements of audit structure is provided by Cronbach's [1951] coefficient alpha. The value of this coefficient for these data is .908. This suggests that our measure of audit structure is highly reliable in the sense that scores for the individual elements of structure are highly correlated with the overall measure.

Audit Methodology Profiles

We shall now develop profiles of the audit methodologies within each of the four categories, commencing with the highly structured category. These profiles provide a more explicit description of the differences in audit structure among the four categories, although they also reveal a few inconsistencies across individual audit structure elements which are not apparent from the summary data in Figure 4.3.

The Highly Structured Audit Methodologies

The two firms whose audit methodologies are highly structured apparently decided several years ago to adopt their approaches, because their materials are extensive and suggest a sizable development effort. Both make extensive use of preprinted forms to provide explicit guidance for all stages of the audit process. Both utilize explicit criteria for evaluating materiality and risk to shape their overall audit approach to each engagement. Both use highly publicized acronyms to describe key aspects of their audit approach. The more highly structured of the two has developed an audit process flowchart which represents its audit approach as a logical series of steps. There is also a subsidiary flowchart which diagrams the firm's approach to internal control evaluation. These flowcharts provide a framework around which the firm's audit manual is organized; that is, each chapter of the manual is keyed to a particular section of the flowchart.

FIGURE 4.3
Average Scores by Category of Audit Structure and Methodology

	Type of Audit Methodology				
Audit Structure Category	**Highly Structured**	**Semi-structured**	**Partially Structured**	**Un-structured**	**Category Average**
A. Overall audit process	4.50	4.25	2.88	2.25	3.50
B. Initial audit planning	4.40	3.25	2.75	2.00	3.07
C. Audit program design	4.83	3.75	2.92	2.17	3.39
D. Control review and evaluation	4.50	3.63	3.00	2.75	3.42
E. Use of audit tools	4.00	3.08	2.67	2.33	2.97
F. Documentation and review	4.00	3.58	2.75	2.33	3.17
Overall average	4.36	3.51	2.81	2.25	3.21

With respect to initial audit planning, both firms place a strong emphasis on this phase of the audit. Both provide detailed guidance on the steps that should be performed with respect to understanding the client's business, identifying critical audit areas, and administering the engagement. Both provide an explicit definition of the staffing responsibilities for each audit engagement. Both have training programs for the development of audit specialists in areas such as EDP and statistical sampling; the specialists are available as needed for more complex engagements. Both firms have specified criteria for quantification of risk levels based on the assessment of internal control. Both develop a preliminary estimate of materiality to guide the auditor in the design of substantive audit procedures. Both have an extensive set of documentaton requirements for audit planning. The primary difference between the two firms in the area of audit planning is that one places a greater emphasis on the use of forms and checklists to guide the auditor through the performance of all the necessary steps.

In the area of audit program design, both firms provide detailed and comprehensive guidance which centers around the use of an extensive package of preprinted materials. A key feature of both approaches is the incorporation of matrices into their guidance for audit program design. One firm provides a series of matrices that relate possible errors and irregularities (within each of several major transaction cycles) to corresponding control conditions, and that provide guidance to the auditor in considering the impact of control weaknesses on the design of substantive tests. The other firm provides a series of matrices relating control conditions and audit objectives to the choice of substantive procedures for each of several accounts or processing cycles. Both provide preprinted audit programs for key audit areas which may be tailored to the requirements of each engagement. Both perform a significant amount of control review and evaluation on all audit engagements, and utilize a sophisticated approach to determining the extent of reliance on internal control and the resulting effect on the nature, extent, and timing of substantive tests. In their guidance on selection of audit tests, both firms differentiate between those tests that are primarily suited for detection of overstatements and those best suited for detection of understatements. Both firms have explicit criteria for sample design which relate sample precision and reliability to the materiality and risk levels established at the planning stage. Thus the firms are very similar with respect to the overall concept of providing detailed guidance on audit program design, although there are numerous differences in the specific form and content of that guidance.

With respect to their review and evaluation of internal control, both firms use highly structured approaches, but their approaches differ substantially. One firm has developed a very sophisticated approach to documenting a client's system of internal control which utilizes a series of flowcharts focusing on the information flows that affect the financial statements. This documentation methodology focuses on the identification of the key controls within each processing system. Preprinted worksheets used in the approach resemble questionnaires or checklists, and guide the auditor in the selection of test procedures based on the conclusions drawn from the control review. The other firm apparently does not prescribe any standard flowcharting techniques, but does rely on the matrices of errors and irregularities and related control conditions mentioned above, plus a sophisticated internal accounting control questionnaire; these tools are designed to guide the auditor in the selection of appropriate compliance and substantive tests.

Both firms make extensive use of specialized audit tools. One firm has developed a sophisticated computer program to assist the auditor in performing analytical review procedures. Both firms use computer-assisted audit techniques for analysis and retrieval of computerized client data. One of the firms provides extensive guidance with respect to the processing of test transactions in a computer-based accounting system. Both firms make extensive use of statistical sampling techniques, and incorporate sample design criteria (e.g., selection of method, risk levels, and tolerable error amounts) which reflect the conclusions reached in earlier stages of the audit.

With regard to documentation and review, both firms provide detailed guidance and audit aids. The guidance consists of requirements for content, preparation, and administration of working papers, and specification of the review responsibilities of each member of the audit team. Audit aids consist of checklists or questionnaires covering both the review of audit work for compliance with generally accepted auditing standards, and the review of financial statements and related disclosures for compliance with generally accepted accounting principles.

In summary, the audit approaches of these two firms match our definition of a structured audit methodology in that they provide a systematic approach to the audit engagement which is supported by a comprehensive and integrated set of audit tools.

The Semistructured Audit Methodologies

The audit methodologies in this category may be distinguished from the more structured ones described previously in that they are not as highly integrated or comprehensive. Some of these firms appear to be committed to the development of a more structured approach, while others appear committed to an approach they believe achieves the advantages of structure without being overly complex and inflexible.

The materials obtained from all of these firms contain a well-developed concept of the firm's overall audit process. Three of the firms use an audit process flowchart to describe their approach. All four have organized their audit manuals and other guidance in a logical and systematic way that is generally consistent with the sequence of steps in their audit processes. Thus, in a broad sense the audit approaches of these four firms are structured, and this is reflected in Figure 4.3 by their average score of 4.25 in the category of "overall audit process." However, in the more specific areas of audit structure, the audit guidance provided by these firms is not as extensive as that of the two highly structured audit methodologies, and this is also reflected in Figure 4.3 by average scores significantly less than 4.0 in audit structure categories B through F.

With respect to audit planning, all four of the firms place a substantial emphasis on formal planning. However, the quality and completeness of each firm's guidance in this area is mixed. The most significant difference among the four firms is that two provide explicit criteria for the establishment of a preliminary estimate of materiality for planning purposes, while the other two provide no guidance whatsoever on this issue.

In the area of audit program design, one of the four firms utilizes a series of preprinted matrices relating audit objectives, error types, and audit procedures to assist the auditor in planning substantive tests; this tool is similar in form and quality to the corresponding matrices that are a central part of the highly structured approaches. The other three firms provide preprinted forms or checklists detailing the available audit techniques. All four of these firms require a significant amount of control review and evaluation work on each audit, and provide detailed guidance for establishing the extent of reliance on internal control. Three of the four have explicit criteria for sample design.

With respect to control review and evaluation, one of the firms uses a very sophisticated approach incorporating flowcharting of transaction flows by cycle, and pre-specified control objectives, control techniques, and associated risks for each control objective that is not achieved. The other firms utilize more traditional approaches involving some combination of flowcharts, narrative descriptions, and internal control questionnaires.

None of the four firms makes use of specialized audit tools to the same extent as the two firms with highly structured approaches. However, each of the four firms provides excellent guidance in one or two of the three audit tool areas of analytical review, computer audit, and statistical sampling. All four of the firms provide good general guidance with respect to documentation and review, but only one provides comprehensive checklists to facilitate the review of both the audit work and the financial statements.

In summary, each of the semistructured audit methodologies reflects a systematic and logical approach to the overall audit process, and each contains some very well developed audit aids. However, in certain areas (which vary from one firm to the next), the guidance provided by these firms is considerably less comprehensive than that of the highly structured methodologies. The general impression gained from studying the semistructured audit methodologies is that these firms believe that structure is worthwhile up to a point which falls short of the very high degree of structure present in the highly structured approaches.

The Partially Structured Audit Methodologies

Four firms were classified as having a partially structured audit methodology. The differences between the audit methodologies of these four firms and the six more structured methodologies are dramatic. This is reflected in Figure 4.3 by the average score of 2.88 assigned to these audit methodologies in Category A (Overall Audit Process), in contrast to average scores of 4.5 and 4.25 for the highly structured and semistructured methodologies. In general, the materials provided to us by these firms do not present an overall concept of the audit process as an aid to audit planning or as a framework for organizing the remainder of their audit guidance. One firm's manual does contain a detailed logic flowchart entitled "Overview of an Audit Engagement," but there is no indication that this is the firm's prescribed approach to carrying out an audit, and the remainder of their audit manual does not closely correspond to the flowchart. Another of the firms provides a short flow diagram of the steps in an audit; this is less detailed than the audit process flowcharts of the other firms in that it includes only major categories of audit steps, but it does correspond to the topical organization of the firm's audit manual. In general, the guidance provided by these firms tends to be qualitative ("when performing this step, consider these factors . . .") rather than analytical ("if these conditions are present, then the following procedures should be considered . . ."). While one of these firms appears to be in the early stages of developing a more structured audit approach, the other three do not appear to be moving in that direction.

All four of these firms include in their materials a detailed list of required planning steps, but none offer any significant package of audit tools or judgment aids to assist in audit planning. None provide any quantitative or analytical criteria for establishing a preliminary estimate of materiality for planning purposes, and only one provides such criteria for establishing overall assurance levels to guide the design of compliance and substantive tests.

With respect to audit program design, one of the firms uses a series of audit program guides listing audit procedures for each major account category; for each procedure, the auditor records 1) who performed the work, and 2) a working paper reference. The other firms provide sample audit programs or lists of audit objectives and procedures for various audit areas. Thus, the extent of use of complex audit tools by these firms for audit program design is very limited.

In the area of control review and evaluation, all four of the firms have developed some form of guidance. For two of the firms it is a relatively sophisticated set of questionnaires.

One requires flowcharting while two others encourage it. Two provide detailed reference material spelling out the attributes of good internal control for each major transaction cycle.

With respect to specialized audit tools, none of these four firms offers anything unusual in their guidance. All of them discuss auditing in an EDP environment. One provides detailed guidance on the use of financial analysis in analytical review, while two others provide general guidance along the lines of SAS 23, and the fourth provides no guidance on analytical review. Three provide specific guidance on the use of statistical sampling, while the fourth offers very limited guidance in this area. With respect to documentation and review requirements, all four of these firms provide specific guidance, but none make extensive use of audit tools to supplement this guidance.

In general, the four firms rated as having partially structured audit methodologies provide good qualitative guidance that makes limited use of technically elaborate audit tools and that is not organized around an overall concept of the audit process. With one possible exception, these firms do not appear to be moving toward the adoption of a more structured audit approach.

The Unstructured Audit Methodologies

There are significant differences between the two audit methodologies that were rated as unstructured. One of the two firms supplied us with a draft copy of materials on their audit approach indicating that they were in the early stages of implementing a more structured approach. The firm has given a name to their audit approach, and has organized their materials around an overview flowchart of the audit process. This firm's approach places a significant emphasis on formal planning. It has developed a very detailed set of internal control questionnaires to assist the auditor in evaluating the impact of internal control on the selection of test procedures. However, this firm's guidance with respect to all other areas of the audit process is limited, and the extent of their use of audit tools other than the internal control questionnaire apparently is limited as well.

In contrast, materials provided by the other firm offered no overall concept of the firm's audit process, and were not organized in any systematic way. However, this firm does use a number of audit tools, including a series of checklists covering virtually all parts of the audit. The firm also provides extensive guidance on the use of statistical sampling, and uses a computer audit software package. The lack of structure in this firm's approach stems from the absence of guidance on how to incorporate these tools into an overall audit strategy, and on how to interpret the results obtained from applying the tools.

In conclusion, the audit approaches of these two firms appear to be of the same general nature as the approaches rated as partially structured. However, they were scored significantly below the partially structured methodologies for different reasons—in one case because of a lack of completeness, and in the other case because of a lack of analytical characteristics.

Summary

Half of the 12 firms in our study use an audit methodology with a relatively high degree of structure, while the other half use a relatively unstructured approach. Based on an examination of publication dates of the various materials provided by each firm, and on receipt of more current materials subsequent to our initial review, we sense that some firms are moving toward a more structured approach, while others are satisfied with the degree of structure present in their existing approach. We received no indication that any of the 12 firms is moving in the direction of a less structured approach.

Advantages and Disadvantages of Audit Structure

The implementation of a more structured audit methodology may have a number of apparent advantages and disadvantages for a CPA firm. This section reviews recent trends in the accounting profession that we believe have encouraged several firms to adopt a more structured auditing approach, and then identifies several possible advantages and disadvantages of such an approach for a CPA firm. We believe that these advantages and disadvantages are generalizable to some extent, but their applicability for any one firm is clearly dependent upon the specific characteristics of that firm.[1] This was made clear to us in discussions and correspondence with the firms' representatives who reviewed an earlier draft of this report.

Advantages

The possible advantages of a structured audit methodology can be traced to several trends that have recently affected the auditing environment. The development of structured audit methodologies to some extent may be viewed as a response on the part of some large accounting firms to these trends. Five major trends are identified here.

First, a trend is evident toward greater competition among large accounting firms, particularly with respect to audit services. Audit clients are rotating auditors more frequently, are becoming more conscious of differences in audit fees and audit quality, and are becoming more thorough in the process of selecting an auditor. In turn, large accounting firms are becoming more aggressive in seeking new audit clients and more competitive in pricing audit services.

Second, there is a trend toward greater regulation of auditing. Not too many years ago the AICPA was the only significant regulatory body of concern to auditors. Now, the AICPA, SEC, FASB, and numerous regulatory bodies in specialized industries must be considered. The auditor must be careful to ensure that all applicable regulatory requirements are being complied with on each audit engagement.

Third, accounting firms are becoming increasingly sensitive to the adverse effects of audit litigation. The volume of such litigation has increased in recent years, and judgments against the auditor in some cases have led to uncertainty regarding the extent of the auditor's responsibilities in certain areas. In response to this trend, auditors have become more concerned that their approach to an audit engagement and their documentation of results are capable of standing up to legal scrutiny.

A fourth trend is toward increasing complexity of data processing technology. Computers are now a pervasive tool for processing accounting data. Furthermore, the variety of computer technology has multiplied substantially, in the form of minicomputers, microcomputers, intelligent terminals, database systems, and data communications networks. Large accounting firms must ensure that their audit personnel are prepared for a wide variety of data processing environments.

A fifth trend involves increased complexity in our economic environment. Service industries have displaced manufacturing as the dominant type of company. Within the

---

[1]Insight into the advantages and disadvantages of structured audit approaches can also be found in the discussion by Dirsmith and McAllister [1982a, 1982b] of mechanistic vs. organic audit strategies.

recent past, inflation and interest rates have exhibited unusually high variability. Business failures are now more common than at any time in recent memory. Corporations are utilizing more complex capital structures involving warrants, convertible securities, and other exotic financial instruments. Mergers and acquisitions occur regularly, and highly diversified companies are a common part of our economic scene. In this environment, the problem of ensuring that financial reporting properly reflects economic reality has become more difficult.

The development of a structured audit methodology may help a large accounting firm respond to these trends. For example, several firms use their audit methodologies as a marketing tool. The name given to the audit approach and some of its key features may form a prominent part of the firm's advertising and marketing strategy. By using its unique auditing approach as a marketing tool, a large accounting firm seeks to differentiate itself from its competitors and gain the respect of clients and potential clients.

In response to price competition, an accounting firm may hope to perform more efficient audits as the result of a more structured approach. The structured audit methodology can free the auditor from many of the more routine tasks involved in organizing the audit approach, and allow the audit team to focus on the specific judgments required for each client. With its focus on systematic selection of audit procedures to accomplish specific objectives, a structured audit methodology may enable the auditor to reduce the number of unnecessary procedures performed.

In response to increased regulation and litigation, a structured audit methodology may facilitate quality control of audit work. Specifically, the structured audit methodology helps to ensure that the same general approach is followed on all audits, which facilitates compliance with generally accepted auditing standards. Furthermore, the structured audit methodology can provide checklists, review procedures, and other techniques which may help ensure compliance with all applicable accounting and auditing standards. Finally, the structured audit methodology can provide a standard format for documenting audit findings and conclusions in a way that will withstand legal scrutiny.

In response to increased technological and economic complexity a structured audit methodology can provide specialized auditing tools to help the auditor understand and cope with unusual audit environments. Examples of such tools presently in use include EDP internal control questionnaires, computer audit software, financial analysis techniques, and financial disclosure checklists. A structured approach also incorporates the use of specialists in audits of complex EDP applications, or in audits of specialized industries.

A structured audit methodology may also facilitate the training of audit staff. Since the methodology is based on a logical sequence of steps, it may be easier for trainees to grasp. Furthermore, as new audit tools are introduced, their rationale can be explained in terms of the overall audit approach, which may facilitate learning and understanding.

Another possible advantage of a structured audit methodology is that it may facilitate communication among auditors within a firm. It provides a common terminology with which all members of the audit team are familiar. This may save audit staff time, and also reduce the possibility of misunderstandings with respect to the requirements of each audit job.

Finally, an accounting firm may adopt a more structured audit methodology because of a belief that the high cost of even infrequent audit failure coupled with the pressures to keep audit costs at a minimum, in a very complex business and technical environment, requires a shift of control of audit decision making away from the individual auditor and toward the central firm.

Disadvantages

In addition to the possible advantages, a structured audit approach also may have several disadvantages. One possible disadvantage is inflexibility. A structured approach may be designed to anticipate specific features of the typical audit environment to such a degree that it cannot be applied easily to atypical audit environments. In turn, this could lead to either of two problems. First, the approach could be inefficient when applied to the atypical audit environment. Second, and more significant, use of the approach may render the auditor ineffective in such environments, leading to failure to meet one or more audit objectives, or even to the formulation of an inappropriate audit opinion.

A structured audit approach could also cause some auditors to be less effective in all audit environments. Whenever there is extensive use of such audit tools as preprinted audit programs, questionnaires, and checklists to provide structure, the auditor may become mechanistic in his or her thinking. This could cause the auditor to fail to observe important facts, or to fail to reason through to appropriate judgments and conclusions.

A structured audit approach also may be inefficient in less complex audit environments. It may force the auditor to perform procedures or create documentation in situations where these steps are not really necessary other than to comply with the requirements of the audit process. Similarly, a particular audit approach may be stressed, such as heavy reliance on controls, when another emphasis may be more efficient in many cases.

It is possible that use of a structured audit methodology could be a disadvantage to an accounting firm subject to litigation concerning an auditing engagement. Because the structured methodology provides a very explicit description of firm policies, it makes the firm potentially more vulnerable to charges that it did not follow its own policies in a given case. A firm whose policies are based on "auditor judgment" could be less vulnerable to such charges.

Still another possible disadvantage of a structured audit approach is its impact on the auditor. Some staff auditors may feel that structured tools reduce their opportunities to exercise discretion and judgment to an unacceptably low level, and shift too much control of audit decision making away from the field auditor. Staff auditors who feel this way may react in one of two ways: They may resist accepting the directives of the structured methodology, or they may simply leave the firm. Over time, as the structured audit methodology becomes ingrained into the culture of the accounting firm, the firm may find that it attracts and retains only those auditors who are comfortable working in a highly structured environment. If those who tend to leave the firm for this reason are the brighter audit staff members who seek more challenging work, while those who tend to stay are less highly qualified, then the firm may suffer adverse consequences in the long run.

Structured audit methodologies may also have an impact upon the distribution of audit staff at various levels within the firm. To the extent that structured tools reduce the time required to perform routine audit work normally performed by junior staff accountants, the relative portion of junior staff accountants within the firm could decline. Structured methodologies generally involve a greater role for specialists in areas such as statistical auditing and computer auditing, and therefore the relative proportion of audit specialists might be expected to grow in a firm which uses a structured approach. Also, structured approaches involve more elaborate quality control and review procedures on the part of audit managers and partners, which could tend to increase the relative proportion of these personnel within the firm. Changes such as these in the distribution of audit personnel at various levels within the firm could present formidable staff management problems for the firm.

Finally, perhaps the most obvious disadvantage of a highly structured audit approach is the cost of developing the approach and the related audit tools, of implementing the approach within a large audit practice, and of monitoring audit personnel firm-wide for compliance with the prescribed audit approach.

Summary and Discussion

The two views of audit structure represented by the above discussion of its possible advantages and disadvantages may appear to be irreconcilable. However, a partial reconciliation may be possible if we adopt a more refined view of what audit structure is. One possible view is that there are two types of structure: *static* and *dynamic*.[2] Static audit structure imposes uniformity, control, and rigidity, but is not adaptive. It might be exemplified by standard audit programs, internal control questionnaires, and fixed sample sizes. This type of audit structure could be subject to most or all of the disadvantages of structure cited previously, and be of limited effectiveness in achieving the advantages of structure.

In contrast, dynamic audit structure also imposes control, but is adaptive rather than rigid and imposes uniformity only in uniform circumstances. This might be exemplified by audit program matrices, flowcharting techniques, sample size formulae, and auditors who are trained to apply these tools appropriately in a variety of circumstances. This type of audit structure could possibly achieve most or all of the advantages cited above, and be less subject to some of the disadvantages.

It is apparent that the six "more structured" audit methodologies we examined contain varying degrees of static and dynamic structure. It may be that differences between firms reflect differing circumstances; e.g., clientele, educational and experiential backgrounds of personnel, and size of firm—and each firm's degree of audit structure may, in fact, be ideal for that firm. It might be that, under certain circumstances, even a dynamically structured audit methodology may have significant disadvantages. This may explain why some firms have not committed themselves to the development of a more structured approach even though several of their competitors have.

Research Implications of Audit Structure

The research implications of structured audit methodologies can be studied at three levels—the macro level, the micro level, and the individual level. At the macro level, numerous characteristics of large accounting firms can be examined with the goal of identifying significant differences between those firms that follow highly structured approaches and those that follow unstructured approaches. At the micro level, field studies can be performed within the two types of firms in order to identify significant impacts of structured approaches. At the individual level, behavioral experiments can be performed to explore the effect of structured audit techniques on the quality of auditor decision making.

Research at the macro and micro levels requires that the large accounting firms be classified according to the degree of structure of their audit methodologies. Unfortunate-

---

[2]This concept was suggested to us by Robert K. Elliott of Peat, Marwick, Mitchell & Co.

ly, our agreement with the firms participating in this study precludes disclosure of our classification results for any of the firms. However, the increasing tendency of accounting firms to disclose information about their audit approaches via journal articles[3] and conference presentations[4] should enable astute observers of the auditing scene to classify many of the large accounting firms with reasonable accuracy.

At the macro level, we might expect to find certain differences between "structured firms" and "unstructured firms." For example, if structured audit methodologies do improve audit efficiency, reduce audit costs, and give the firm a more distinct image in the marketplace, as their proponents claim, then we might expect to see structured firms gaining audit clients and audit revenues at the expense of unstructured firms. If structured approaches work best on larger and more typical audit clients, then we might expect to see the clientele of structured firms evolve in this direction, while the clientele of unstructured firms evolves toward smaller and more atypical audit clients. If structured audit approaches are really more effective in controlling audit risk, then we might expect to see relatively fewer structured firms as objects of audit litigation. If structured audit approaches do affect the distribution of audit staff at various levels, then we might expect to see significant changes in partner/staff ratios within the structured firms.

Field studies within structured and unstructured firms should also address some interesting issues. For example, detailed studies of the time spent by audit personnel on different types of activities, such as information gathering, information analysis, consultation with client personnel, consultation with other audit staff, preparation or review of documentation, etc., could reveal whether there are significant differences in the distribution of time among these activities that may be attributable to differences in the degree of audit structure employed. Also, attitudes, opinions, and satisfaction measures of audit personnel at various staff levels could be obtained to see whether there are significant differences in these measures between structured and unstructured firms. Personality and cognitive characteristics of audit staff could be evaluated to assess whether there are significant differences in the types of auditors attracted to and retained by structured firms. Working papers could be reviewed to evaluate the extent to which audit staff in structured firms are using the structured methodology and complying with its requirements and recommendations.

Behavioral studies in laboratory settings could test the impact of structured techniques on auditor decision making. For example, the extent to which structured techniques increase consistency and consensus among auditors in making various audit decisions could be examined. Researchers might also examine whether structured techniques reduce the average time required to perform certain audit tasks. Also of interest is whether the use of structured techniques influences actual audit decisions concerning the nature, extent, or timing of planned audit procedures, or conclusions about the meaning of audit evidence.

Summary

A structured audit methodology is a systematic approach to auditing characterized by

---

[3]For example, see Elliott [1983], Grobstein and Craig [1984], Mock and Willingham [1983], and Stringer [1975].

[4]For example, see Mullarkey [1984] and Sullivan [1984].

a prescribed, logical sequence of procedures, decisions, and documentation steps, and by a comprehensive and integrated set of audit policies and tools designed to assist the auditor in conducting the audit. This chapter describes a method of measuring the degree of structure in a firm's audit approach. We applied this method to the audit methodologies of our 12 subject firms and concluded that six of them are using a structured approach. Numerous possible advantages and disadvantages of structured audit methodologies were identified and discussed. Additional research on this and other aspects of audit structure should be conducted before any definitive conclusions may be reached regarding the audit approaches which work best in a particular set of circumstances.

CHAPTER FIVE

Conclusions and Recommendations

This study is descriptive in nature. Until a basic understanding of how auditing is done has been obtained, it is not possible to develop testable hypotheses concerning the audit process. Therefore, the results of our study are in the form of detailed observations concerning the audit methodologies of the participating firms, presented in Chapters 3 and 4, and recommendations concerning the implications of our findings, presented in this chapter. Our recommendations are of two types: overall recommendations based on our experience in performing the study, and detailed recommendations and observations that flow from the cross-firm analysis presented in Chapter 3.

Overall Recommendations

1. *We recommend that the Auditing Standards Board reorganize and maintain the SASs in a format consistent with the flow of the audit process.* It is our assumption that the SASs are used to provide guidance to, and to serve as a reference for, auditors in designing and conducting audit examinations. As auditing pronouncements have been written and published, they have been organized in a topical manner. This topical organization is significantly different than the audit process format of most firms' materials. Thus, it would be difficult for auditors using those materials to relate specific steps to the professional literature, and the professional literature to specific steps. As an indication of this, one need only refer to Chapter 2 where paragraphs from the SASs are cross-referenced to the normative GAAS model developed.

In a similar vein, we note that the trend among the firms in the study has been toward audit methodologies that follow a logical, step-by-step process. It is anticipated that other accounting firms may follow this trend. A restructuring of the literature would help in this task.

Finally, we believe that the problem of organizing the professional auditing literature has arisen partly because of rapid expansion of the literature. Given the present number of SASs and the probability of continued expansion, a process-oriented framework might be desirable simply to accommodate more information.

2. *We recommend that firm materials be used by the AICPA as a research and development database.* We found the materials we reviewed to be of extremely high quality, without exception. One could say that this collection of materials represents the best literature on auditing available. This should not be too surprising, because each of the 12 firms has a staff of highly qualified persons responsible for developing their materials and presenting them in appropriate form for implementation.

We also noted that the materials across the firms complement each other. That is, different areas have received special emphasis by different firms. Thus, many audit topics and areas have received an intensive investigation by at least one of the firms. This adds to the collective strength of all the materials.

As we understand the standard-setting process, a great deal of the detailed work is done at the task force level. A particular task force will be staffed by persons from several firms and will be supported by an AICPA staff person. Whether the task force will include representatives of the firms that have given the most study to the topic at hand may be a matter of coincidence, or at least difficult to administer.

We recommend that a copy of each firm's materials be entrusted to the Institute to serve as a research database for Auditing Standards Board projects. It would be controlled to protect concerns about confidentiality, but would be available to the task force support staff person so that the best materals developed by the profession would be available to the task force in its efforts. It could also serve as a basis for selection of task force firm representation.

3. *We recommend that auditing researchers and practitioners give more formal consideration to the structure question.* We have come to believe that how the audit process is implemented is clearly as important as how it is logically designed. In Chapter 4 we describe several potential advantages and disadvantages relating to the degree of structure a firm selects. It would appear that there is a trade-off involved: adding structure may bring advantages to a point, and then too much structure may bring disadvantages. Of course, the method by which structure is achieved will significantly affect this. Thus, each firm must seek to arrive at the optimum point of structure for that firm and give careful consideration to the methods it uses.

The question of structure is complex and should be studied and subjected to formal research. We have identified 18 elements of a firm's audit methodology which we use to measure structure. Are these the appropriate elements? To what degree is the question of structure firm-specific? What correlations exist between the degree of structure and various measures of firm success?

We further believe that the nature of these types of questions is such that the related research must be done at the firm and/or professional level. A significant number of firms must participate, and data about the firm as a whole (some of it sensitive) must be obtained. It is unlikely that one or a few academic researchers could accomplish much in this area on an *ad hoc* basis. However, an Auditing Standards Board-sponsored effort could certainly succeed to the benefit of all constitutent firms.

Detailed Recommendations and Observations

Chapter 3 presents a detailed analysis of the firms' audit methodologies by audit process step. This analysis focuses on 1) instances where nonconformity with the GAAS model exists, and 2) instances where firm requirements go beyond GAAS.

We believe that the most important findings are of the first case. They imply either that the requirements of professional standards are onerous in some way and not acceptable to practitioners, in which case the requirements should be reviewed, or that the firms' guidance is at a substandard level in some respects. In the second case, the implication is that practice precedes standards in many areas and/or that standards are considered to be a floor for performance, not a ceiling.

In this section we summarize our findings by the above two categories. To put this summary in the proper perspective, we must preface it by saying that, with the possible exception of one subparagraph of SAS No. 22, dealing with the consideration of preliminary estimates of materiality levels for planning purposes, all of the 12 sets of firm materials are substantively in conformity with GAAS. Furthermore, the only items mentioned in this summary are those that were present or absent in a significant number of the firm materials. In the detailed analysis in Chapter 3, several additional items are described which involve only one or two firms.

1. Instances of non-conformity
   a. *Preliminary Estimation of Materiality*. Five of the 12 sets of firm materials do not

contain guidance with respect to the requirement that, during planning, the auditor should consider preliminary estimates of materiality. We recognize that this requirement is re-emphasized in the recent exposure draft on materiality and risk (subsequently issued as SAS 47). We have not studied this problem in detail, but we suspect that auditors may have the following concerns:

i. They are unwilling to be explicit about defining a materiality number during planning that may not be appropriate when judgments are made about the presentation of the financial statements during the final stages of the audit.

ii. They are unable or unwilling to specify a materiality number in the absence of some generally accepted criteria for determining the amount (although we note that SAS 22 does not require that a numerical estimate be made).

We have reviewed SAS 47 in light of these two concerns. It appears that it is helpful regarding the first concern to some degree, but of little help with the second. Of course, any help offered by the new standards may not obviate auditor fears stemming from potential litigation and regulatory matters.

b. *Compliance testing.* There is significant disagreement among the firms on what constitutes a compliance test and how such tests are performed. This does not necessarily represent nonconformance with GAAS, but rather, a lack of clarity or acceptance of what GAAS requires. Specifically:

i. Eight of the 12 firms effectively require reperformance of accounting steps as part of detailed compliance tests. The remaining four firms identify such activity as substantive in nature.

ii. There is a disagreement on the worth of observation compliance tests. One firm argues that they are less reliable than transaction tests and one firm argues the opposite position.

iii. Two firms have abandoned the terminology in the SAS for compliance tests and have adopted other terms that they feel are more descriptive of what is actually being done.

iv. Four of the firms cycle tests among areas over a period of audit years. In other words, they don't test all controls that they rely on to the same extent every year.

v. In performing compliance tests, five firms strongly encourage or require the use of statistical sampling.

2. Instances where firm requirements go beyond GAAS.

a. *Engagement letters* are required by all 12 firms, even though they are not required by GAAS.

b. There is a *bias toward reliance on internal control* in the policies and materials of eight of the 12 firms. We interpret GAAS as permitting reliance if controls are adequate for that purpose. These firms seem to believe reliance is superior to a substantive approach if the choice exists.

c. *Transaction walk-throughs* are required by six of the 12 firms. They are mentioned but not required by GAAS.

d. Many of the firms give great emphasis to the use of *advanced auditing techniques*; these would include: statistical sampling (see 1.b.v above), computer-assisted auditing, analytical review methods, and techniques for linking the various segments of the audit.

e. Whereas the professional literature does not speak to the practical details and administrative aspects of *drafting and issuing the auditor's report,* these matters were covered extensively in the firms' materials.

f. *Other matters* included in firm materials but not included in GAAS are:
  i. Engagement administration
  ii. Engagement team meetings
  iii. Engagement budgeting procedures
  iv. Staff appraisal procedures
  v. Retention of working papers

In conclusion, the materials we reviewed provide a revealing look at how the auditing process is viewed by the large accounting firms. The consistently good quality of the materials is reassuring, as is the indication that all of the materials are substantially in compliance with GAAS. The trend within some firms toward the implementation of a more structured approach to the auditing process is an intriguing development that deserves additional consideration by auditing researchers and practitioners, and perhaps by the Auditing Standards Board. Finally, we believe that the materials provided to us by the 12 participating firms represent a database of auditing guidance of unsurpassed quality that should be preserved and maintained as reference material for those involved in establishing auditing standards.

APPENDIX A

Detailed GAAS References in Support of Audit Process Model

This appendix contains our list of GAAS references, organized according to our audit process outline in Figure 2.1. Some of the entries are direct quotes, while others are paraphrased, but each is accompanied by a reference to the SAS section and paragraph from which it was obtained.

A key to the reference codes used in this Appendix is as follows:

AU — Codification of Statements on Auditing Standards Numbers 1 to 26 (AICPA, 1980)
Omnibus — draft of Omnibus Statement on Auditing Standards, subsequently issued as SAS 43.
SAS — Statement on Auditing Standards
SQCS — Statement on Quality Control Standards

1.0 PRE-ENGAGEMENT ACTIVITIES

1.1 ACCEPT/REJECT NEW CLIENT

Reference	Description
SQCS 1 P 7h	Procedures should be employed to determine the acceptability of a potential new client.
AU 315.04-315.05	When the audit is a new engagement, information should be obtained from the previous auditor in determining whether to accept the engagement.

1.2 ESTABLISH TERMS OF ENGAGEMENT

Reference	Description
(No references)	

1.3 ASSIGNMENT OF STAFF

Reference	Description
SQCS 1 P 7b AU 210.01	Persons should be assigned to the engagement who have the degree of technical training and proficiency required in the circumstances.

2.0 PLANNING ACTIVITIES

Reference	Description
AU 310.01	There must be adequate planning.

AU 311.03	Planning involves developing an overall strategy, considering pertinent available data.
AU 327.05, 327.06	The auditor should plan his examination with an attitude of professional skepticism, recognizing his responsibility to search for errors and irregularities that would have a material effect on the financial statements.
AU 311.04	Specific procedures should be performed to accomplish planning.
AU 311.04	The results of the planning process may be documented by memorandum.
AU 311.02	Portions of planning can be delegated to engagement personnel.
AU 321.02, 321.04	Special considerations, including approach and staffing, exist when the client uses EDP.
AU 322.01	The work of internal auditors should be considered in developing the audit approach.

2.1 OBTAIN KNOWLEDGE OF THE BUSINESS

Reference	**Description**
AU 311.06, 311.07, 331.03	The auditor should obtain adequate knowledge of the client's business and industry. This knowledge is used in planning and throughout the examination.
AU 335.10	This should include an understanding of management responsibilities and the relationship of each component to the entire entity.
AU 311.08, 311.04	The auditor's knowledge of the business is acquired through inquiries, inspection of documents, observation, use of reference materials, and consultation with persons who are informed about the industry.

2.11 PRELIMINARY ANALYTICAL REVIEW

Reference	**Description**
AU 318.05	Analytical review procedures may be performed in the planning phase to assist in determining the audit strategy.

2.12 APPRAISAL OF RISK

Reference	Description
AU 311.03, 311.06	In planning his examination, the auditor should identify and consider areas requiring special attention, financial statement items likely to require adjustment, and conditions that may require extension or modification of audit tests.
AU 150.05	The auditor should consider the degree of risk associated with major types of transactions and accounts in order that relatively more audit effort may be devoted to areas of higher risk.
AU 335.11	The auditor should be aware of transactions with related parties which require special consideration.
AU 315.06-315.09	When the audit is a new engagement, information should be obtained from the previous auditor regarding: • facts that might bear on the integrity of management; • disagreements with management as to accounting principles, auditing procedures, or other significant matters; • the previous auditor's understanding as to the reasons for the change of auditors; and • matters that the successor believes may affect the conduct of his examination. (Note: These procedures are performed when considering the acceptability of a potential new client. However, once the decision to accept is made, the information assists in the appraisal of risk.)

2.2 PRELIMINARY ESTIMATION OF MATERIALITY

Reference	Description
AU 150.04	There should be stronger grounds to sustain the auditor's opinion with respect to those items which are relatively more important and with respect to those in which the possibilities of material error are greater than with respect to those of lesser importance or those in which the possibility of material error is remote.
AU 311.03	During planning, the auditor should establish preliminary estimates of materiality levels. These will be used in:

	• Developing the overall audit strategy.
SAS 39 P 18	• Establishing tolerable error levels in planning samples for substantive tests.
AU 337.12	• Reaching an understanding with attorneys for purposes of responding re: litigation matters.
AU 435.05	• Planning allocation of audit work to segments in publicly held entities.

2.3 REVIEW OF INTERNAL ACCOUNTING CONTROL

Reference	Description
AU 320.01, 320.08 Omnibus .52	Every audit should include a study and evaluation of internal control. At a minimum, this shall include obtaining an understanding of the control environment and the flow of transactions. Documentation may be limited to a record of the auditor's reasons for deciding not to extend his review past the minimum level.
AU 320.49	The study and evaluation relates to accounting controls (i.e., does not include administrative controls.)
AU 320.28	Internal accounting control should provide reasonable assurance that four broad objectives are met within the entity: 1. Transactions are executed in accordance with management's general or specific authorization. 2. Transactions are recorded as necessary (1) to permit preparation of financial statements in conformity with generally accepted accounting principles or any other criteria applicable to such statements, and (2) to maintain accountability for assets. 3. Access to assets is permitted only in accordance with management's authorization. 4. The recorded accountability for assets is compared with the existing assets at reasonable intervals and appropriate action is taken with respect to any differences.
SAS 30 P23 & 24 AU 320.21 320.35-39 320.42, 320.45	A number of specific characteristics can be identified with a system that meets the above objectives. These would be understood by the auditor.

Omnibus .51	The purpose of the review of the system is to obtain sufficient knowledge and understanding about the accounting system and the internal accounting control system: (a) to make a determination of whether there are internal accounting control procedures that may provide a basis for reliance thereon in determining the nature, extent, and timing of substantive tests; or (b) to aid the auditor in designing substantive tests in the absence of such reliance.
Omnibus .52, .53	The auditor's review may be done in two stages—a preliminary phase, which is required for material classes of transactions, and a completion of the review performed only in those areas where reliance on internal control is planned.
AU 321.24	Where EDP is used, the auditor's review should encompass both the manual and EDP portions of the system.
AU 322.04	Where internal audit exists, the function should be included in the auditor's understanding of the system.
AU 327.07	In evaluating internal control, the auditor uses accumulated experience and understanding of the points of risk for possible errors and irregularities.
AU 327.09, 327.10	The auditor should recognize that management can override internal controls and should be aware of the importance of management integrity.
AU 328.13	Where an illegal act is determined to exist, the auditor should consider the implications in relation to his reliance on internal control and the representations of management.
AU 335.10	The auditor should evaluate internal accounting control over management activities and he should consider the business purpose served by the various components of the entity.

2.31 PRELIMINARY PHASE

Reference	**Description**
Omnibus .52	The preliminary phase of such a review should be designed to provide the auditor with an understanding of the control environment and the flow of transactions through the accounting system.
AU 321.25	Where EDP is used, this should include the extent to which EDP is used.

Omnibus .53	On completion of the preliminary phase, an auditor may conclude that further study and evaluation are unlikely to justify any restriction of substantive tests. An auditor may also conclude that the audit effort required to study and evaluate the design of the system and to test compliance with prescribed control procedures, to justify reliance on them to restrict the extent of substantive tests, exceeds the reduction in audit effort that could be achieved by such reliance. Either conclusion would cause an auditor to discontinue further study and evaluation of the internal accounting control system and to design substantive tests that do not contemplate reliance on such internal accounting control procedures.

2.32 COMPLETION PHASE

Reference	**Description**
Omnibus .55	If, after completion of the preliminary phase of the review, the auditor plans to rely on the system, he would complete the review.
AU 320.65	The auditor, in reviewing and evaluating internal accounting control, should:
	1. Consider the types of errors and irregularities that could occur.
	2. Determine the accounting control procedures that should prevent or detect such errors and irregularities.
	3. Determine whether the necessary control procedures are prescribed.
SAS 30 P 18	This is conducted in several steps:
SAS 30 P21	1. Identify specific control objectives for specific classes of transactions.
SAS 30 P 22	2. Identify existing control procedures for the system description which relate to those objectives.
AU 320.54	3. Make a preliminary evaluation of whether the objectives should be met by the controls, assuming satisfactory compliance with them.
SAS 30 P 30-32	In so doing, the auditor is interested in identifying material weaknesses in internal control.

AU 320.01, 320.34	The results of the review of internal accounting control will be used to refine the audit strategy being developed. It should be noted that because any system, no matter how well designed, has certain limitations, there is a limit to the extent it can be relied upon.
AU 321.07	When general EDP controls are weak or absent, the auditor should consider the effect of such weaknesses or absence in the evaluation of application controls.
AU 322.06-08	Procedures should be followed to review the competence and objectivity of, and evaluate the work of, internal auditors, where they are providing assistance and/or being relied upon as part of the internal accounting control system.
Omnibus .56	The auditor may trace one or a few transactions through the system to clarify his understanding and description of the system.

2.4 DEVELOP OVERALL AUDIT PLAN

Reference	**Description**
AU 311.03	The auditor will develop an overall strategy for the examination.
AU 320.01, 320.08, 320.50 & 51 SAS 30 P 10 AU 321.26	The strategy will include: • The extent to which internal control will be relied upon.
AU 320.55 SAS 30 P 15 AU 310.05	• The nature, extent, and timing of tests of compliance.
AU 320.71, 320.69, 320.70, 320.73	• The nature, extent, and timing of substantive tests.
AU 311.04 AU 322.10	• Staffing requirements and the extent of involvement of consultants, specialists, and internal auditors.

AU 311.03d	• Preliminary estimates of materiality for audit purposes.
SAS 31 P 9	• Specific audit objectives in light of assertions embodied in the financial statements.
AU 311.04	The strategy—or preliminary audit plan—may be documented by memorandum.
AU 320.50 SAS 39 P 43	Some tests will often be designed to obtain both compliance and substantive evidence.
SAS 39 P 43	Where this is done, sample size should be the larger of the samples that would otherwise have been designed for the two separate purposes.
AU 310.05	The tests can be performed at various times during the year.
AU 336.04-.08	The examination may involve use of a specialist. This will require that the auditor satisfy himself as to the professional qualifications and reputation of the specialist, reach an understanding on the nature of the work to be performed, and determine whether the findings of the specialist are suitable for the auditor's purpose.

2.41 DETERMINE APPROPRIATE RELIANCE ON INTERNAL ACCOUNTING CONTROL

Reference	Description
AU 320.55 (see omnibus for new wording)	The auditor may decide not to perform tests of compliance for either of the following reasons: (1) prescribed internal accounting controls are judged not satisfactory for reliance thereon, or (2) the audit effort required to test compliance with the procedures to justify reliance on them in making substantive tests would exceed the reduction in effort that could be achieved by such reliance.
AU 320.71	The second standard of field work does not contemplate that the auditor will place complete reliance on internal control to the exclusion of other auditing procedures with respect to material amounts in the financial statements.

2.42 DESIGN COMPLIANCE TESTING PROCEDURES

Reference	Description
AU 320.55 SAS 30 P 25 AU 320.57	Compliance tests will be performed to provide evidence that the specific control procedures to be relied upon are operating as prescribed.
AU 320.60	The purpose of tests of compliance is to provide a reasonable degree of assurance, which is a matter of audit judgment.
AU 320.56, 320.58 SAS 39 P 35	Where the controls require documented evidence of performance, the auditor will inspect that evidence.
AU 320.61 SAS 39 P 38	• These tests should ideally be performed on data for the entire period, but can be done through an interim date with appropriate procedures to year end.
AU 320.61	• Samples, if any, can be on a statistical or nonstatistical basis.
SAS 39 P 31, 33, 34, 36 & 37	• Sample design should consider: (1) The audit objective (2) The maximum rate of compliance deviation that would support planned reliance (3) Allowable sampling risk of over- and under-reliance—the risk of overreliance should be controlled at a low level (4) Characteristics of the population.
AU 320.59, 320.63, 320.52	Where controls leave no documentary evidence of performance, the auditor will obtain evidence of compliance with inquiry and observation.
	• Observations will be made while the auditor is present on the client's premises conducting other phases of the audit.
	• Procedures to trace transactions to clarify the understanding and description of the system can be used in making observations.
AU 321.29	• Certain types of EDP controls that leave no visible audit trail may require the review of transactions, either manually or through the use of EDP.

AU 322.06 - 08	When internal audit is being relied upon as an internal accounting control, the auditor must consider the competence and objectivity of internal auditors and test their work to evaluate their performance. The work of internal auditors may be tested by reperformance or comparison of the results of tests by internal auditors with parallel tests of the independent auditor.
AU 310.06	Where tests of compliance are done through an interim date, the auditor must satisfy himself that internal control procedures are still effective at year-end.

2.43 DESIGN SUBSTANTIVE PROCEDURES

Reference	**Description**
AU 320.70	The evidential matter required by the third standard is obtained through two general classes of auditing procedures: (a) tests of details of transactions and balances, and (b) analytical review procedures applied to financial information. These procedures are referred to as "substantive tests." The purpose of these procedures is to obtain evidence as to the validity and propriety of accounting treatment of transactions and balances or, conversely, of errors or irregularities therein.
AU 310.05, 310.06	Those tests may be performed as of interim dates. When this is done, procedures must be performed relating to the period to year-end. Where internal control is good, these may be primarily analytical review procedures.
SAS 31 P 1, 2	The auditor must be assured that his substantive procedures provide sufficient competent evidential matter as a basis for his opinion. Such evidence will be obtained through inspection, observation, inquiries, and confirmations.
SAS 31 P 3 - 10	In designing the audit procedures to obtain sufficient competent evidential matter, the auditor establishes audit objectives for each account balance based on the assertions that are embodied in the financial statement components. The categories of these assertions are: • existence or occurrence • completeness • rights and obligations • valuation or allocation • presentation and disclosure
SAS 31 P 10 - 12	In selecting particular substantive tests, the auditor considers:

- his reliance on internal control
- relative risk of material errors or irregularities
- specific audit objectives
- efficiency and effectiveness of tests
- available evidential matter

SAS 31
P 13 - 18

Evidential matter can be divided into two classes: (1) the client's underlying accounting data and related records and documents, and (2) corroborating information, which includes documentary material such as checks, invoices, contracts, written representations, and information obtained by examining assets, observing functions and activities, making inquiries, computations and analyses, and obtaining confirmations from outside parties.

SAS 31
P 19 - 21

Evidential matter will generally be persuasive rather than convincing. The auditor will gather evidence in such a way that there is a rational relationship between the cost of evidence and its usefulness; but in any case, the auditor must decide whether the evidence gathered within the limits of time and cost is sufficient to justify his opinion.

AU
320.75
SAS 39
P 4, 8, 9,
12, 19, 21

The notion of reasonable cost of evidence supports the use of sampling. Either statistical or nonstatistical sampling is appropriate. In using sampling, the auditor recognizes the concept of sampling risk:

- Ultimate risk is a combination of the risk that (1) material errors will occur, and (2) not be detected by the auditor.
- The auditor relies on internal control to reduce the first risk and on substantive tests to reduce the second risk.
- Where sampling is used, sampling risk—which includes both the risk of incorrect acceptance and the risk of incorrect rejection—is controlled as part of controlling ultimate risk. The larger the sample is, the lower sampling risk.
- Nonsampling risk relates to the effectiveness of audit procedures and proper performance. This is controlled by planning, supervision, and other quality control procedures.

Substantive tests of details of transactions or balances involving sampling may be on a statistical or nonstatistical basis.

In designing the sample:

SAS 39
P 12 & 21

- The auditor should consider sampling risk. Items where acceptance of sampling risk is not justified should be determined and examined 100 percent.

SAS 39
P 24 & 17

- The sample should be selected from the entire population; i.e., the sample should be representative.

SAS 39
P 16, 18, 19 & 23

- The auditor should consider the following factors:
  (1) The audit objectives of the test.
  (2) Preliminary estimates of materiality levels.
  (3) Allowable sampling risk; i.e., the risk of incorrect acceptance and the risk of incorrect rejection—where no reliance is being placed on internal control and other substantive tests, the risk of incorrect acceptance should be low.
  (4) Characteristics of the population.

AU
320.70, 318.02,
318.01, 318.03,
318.06

Analytical review procedures are substantive tests involving a study and comparison of relationships among data. The extent of analytical review procedures is a matter of auditor judgment—no specific analytical review procedures are required.

AU
318.07, 318.09,
310.05, 318.05

Analytical review procedures may be applied to overall financial information or detailed components. They may be applied at different times during the year. In deciding the nature, extent, and timing of the procedures, the auditor should consider:

1. The nature of the entity.
2. The scope of the engagement.
3. The availability of financial information about the entity.
4. The availability of relevant nonfinancial information.
5. The reliability of financial and nonfinancial information.
6. The availability of comparable industry information.

AU
435.07

Analytical review procedures apply to segment information that is presented in the financial statements.

The auditor's examination will include certain generally accepted procedures:

AU
331.01

- Confirmation of accounts receivable.

331.09, 331.10

- Observation of inventories.

332.02

- Audit of proper handling of long-term investments.

331.01-.08

- Obtaining a certain representation from direct management.

337.04

- Obtaining evidence re: litigation, claims, and assessments.

420.14	• (When a first examination) to establish consistent application of accounting principles.
435.05, 435.06	• (For publicly held entities) review of segment information.
SAS 27, P 6 SAS 28, P 4 SAS 33, P 2	• Review of supplementary information required by FASB or SEC.*
AU 335.13-15	• Identifying and examining related-party transactions.
SAS 36 P 24-25	• Review of interim financial information.*
AU 335.12	The auditor should place emphasis on auditing material transactions with parties he knows are related to the entity. This involves specific procedures designed to:
AU 335.12	(1) Determine the existence of related parties.
AU 335.13	(2) Identify material transactions with the parties.
AU 335.14, 335.15	(3) Determine the substance and proper handling of the transactions.

2.44 WRITE AUDIT PROGRAM

Reference	**Description**
AU 311.05	There should be a written audit program.

3.0 COMPLIANCE TESTING ACTIVITIES

3.1 CONDUCT TESTS OF COMPLIANCE

Reference	**Description**
AU 320.57	Tests of compliance are concerned primarily with these questions:

* Note: These reviews are technically not substantive tests. However, they are required and performed in conjunction with substantive tests. Therefore, they are included in this section.

1. Were the necessary procedures performed?
2. How were they performed?
3. By whom were they performed?

SAS 39 P 25 & 29	Audit procedures should be applied to each sample item selected. Where this cannot be done, and to assume the items are in error would imply a material error, alternative procedures must be sought. The implications of not being able to examine items should also be determined and considered.

3.2 FINAL EVALUATION OF INTERNAL ACCOUNTING CONTROL

Reference	**Description**
AU 320.65, 320.66, 320.67, 320.68 SAS 39 P 42	Internal control will be evaluated ("Final") for each significant class of transactions where reliance is planned by identifying types of errors and irregularities not covered by existing control procedures, or covered by existing control procedures with which there is not adequate compliance. In this latter case, planned substantive tests should be altered.
SAS 39 P 32, 40, 41	The adequacy of compliance should consider the frequency of deviations from prescribed procedures and the qualitative aspects of the deviations. The deviation rate in the sample used for a compliance test should be used as the estimate for the population.
AU 321.31	Evaluation of the EDP aspects of the system should be an integral part of the auditor's evaluation of the system of internal accounting control. Accounting control procedures performed both within the EDP activity and by user departments should be considered together by the auditor.

4.0 SUBSTANTIVE TESTING ACTIVITIES

4.1 CONDUCT SUBSTANTIVE TESTS OF TRANSACTIONS

Reference	**Description**
SAS 39 P 25 & 39	Audit procedures should be applied to each sample item selected. Where this cannot be done, and to assume the items are in error would imply a material error, alternative procedures must be sought. The implications of not being able to examine items should also be determined and considered.

4.2 CONDUCT ANALYTICAL REVIEW PROCEDURES

Reference	Description
AU 318.04, 318.08	When the analytical review procedures identify fluctuations that are not expected, or the absence of fluctuations when they are expected, or other items that appear to be unusual, such fluctuations should be investigated by the application of appropriate procedures.
AU 318.08	The auditor's investigation normally begins with suitable inquiries of management. The auditor then evaluates the reasonableness of management's response, and then considers whether other auditing procedures are necessary.
AU 318.08	In investigating significant fluctuations, the auditor should be alert to the possible effects of his findings on his examination of other accounts.

4.3 CONDUCT TESTS OF DETAILS OF BALANCES

Reference	Description
SAS 39 P 25	The audit procedures should be applied to all sample items selected. Where this cannot be done, and to assume the items are in error would imply a material error, alternative procedures must be sought. The implications of not being able to examine items should also be determined and considered.

4.4 POST-BALANCE-SHEET REVIEW PROCEDURES

Reference	Description
AU 560.10, 560.03, 560.05	The auditor must perform procedures applicable to the period from the balance sheet date to the date of his report for the purpose of determining whether any events have occurred during that period which: 1. Provide additional evidence with respect to estimates reflected in the financial statements. 2. Should be disclosed to keep the financial statements from becoming misleading.
AU 560.11	Specific procedures are applied to transactions occurring after the balance sheet date such as: (a) the examination of data to assure that proper cutoffs have been made, and (b) the examination of data which provide information to aid the auditor in his evaluation of assets and liabilities as of the balance sheet date.

AU 560.12	Other procedures to be performed at or near completion of field work should include: 1. Reading interim statements. 2. Making inquiries of management. 3. Reading minutes. 4. Making inquiries of counsel.
AU 33.04-.06, 33.09 SAS 34 P 7, 8, & 9	5. Obtaining certain representations from client management. 6. (Where going-concern is a problem) Review of management plans and supporting projections for future continuation, and discussion of possible legal implications, if any, with appropriate legal counsel, if necessary.

4.5 EVALUATE RESULTS OF SUBSTANTIVE PROCEDURES

Reference	Description
AU 327.08, 327.11, 327.12	In evaluating audit results, the auditor must look for circumstances which indicate that material errors or possible irregularities exist, and pursue these circumstances to his satisfaction.
SAS 39 P 26, 27, 28	In evaluating substantive tests, the error results in the sample should be projected to the population. Total projected and other errors are summed for each objective to determine their effect on the financial statements. Also, the qualitative aspects are considered and the audit strategy is revised if indicated.
AU 335.16	With regard to all related-party transactions, the auditor should evaluate all information available to him to be satisfied that the transactions are adequately disclosed.

4.51 AGGREGATE FINDINGS

Reference	Description
SAS 39 P 29	The auditor will combine all relevant audit evidence in forming a conclusion about an account balance or class of transactions.
SAS 39 P 30	Projected error results for all audit sampling applications and all known errors for nonsampling applications should be considered in the aggregate along with other relevant audit evidence........

4.52 MAKE EVALUATION

Reference	Description
SAS 39 P 30	. . . the auditor evaluates whether the financial statements taken as a whole may be materially misstated.
SAS 39 P 27	In addition to the evaluation of the frequency and amounts of monetary misstatements, consideration should be given to the qualitative aspects of the errors. These include (a) the nature and cause of misstatements . . . , and (b) the possible relationship of the misstatements to other phases of the audit. The discovery of an irregularity ordinarily requires a broader consideration of possible implications than does the discovery of an error.

4.53 MODIFY AUDIT PLAN

Reference	Description
SAS 39 P 28	If the sample results suggest that the auditor's planning assumptions were in error, he should take appropriate action, including altering his evaluation of internal accounting control as a basis for reliance, and modifying other substantive tests that were designed with reliance on those controls, if such modifications are appropriate.

4.6 OBTAIN REPRESENTATIONS

4.61 MANAGEMENT REPRESENTATIONS

Reference	Description
AU 333.01	As part of an examination made in accordance with generally accepted auditing standards, the auditor should obtain certain written representations from management.
AU 333.04, 333.06 - 08	The specific written representations obtained by the auditor will depend on the circumstances of the engagement and the nature and basis of presentation of the financial statements (see list in SAS Section 333).
AU 333.05	Management's representations may be limited to matters that are considered either individually or collectively material to the financial statements, provided management and the auditor have reached an understanding on the limits of materiality for this purpose.

AU 333.09	The letter of representation should be dated as of the date of the auditor's report.

4.62 ATTORNEY'S REPRESENTATIONS

Reference	Description
AU 337.08	A letter of audit inquiry to the client's lawyer is the auditor's primary means of obtaining corroboration of the information furnished by management concerning litigation, claims, and assessments.
AU 337.09	Specific matters should be covered in a letter of audit inquiry. Inquiry need not be made concerning matters that are not considered material, provided the client and the auditor have reached an understanding on the limits of materiality for this purpose.
AU 337.13	A lawyer's refusal to furnish the information requested in an inquiry letter, either in writing or orally, would be a limitation on the scope of the auditor's examination sufficient to preclude an unqualified opinion.

4.63 OTHER REPRESENTATIONS

Reference	Description
(No references)	

5.0 OPINION FORMULATION AND REPORTING ACTIVITIES

5.1 REVIEW FINANCIAL STATEMENTS

Reference	Description
AU 318.05	The auditor may apply analytical review procedures as an overall review of the financial statements.
AU 550.04	Where other information is included in a document containing financial statements, the auditor should read the information to be sure it is not inconsistent with the financial statements.
AU 335.17	Specific financial statement disclosures are required for reporting material related-party transactions.

AU 546.04	The auditor should evaluate a change in accounting principle to satisfy himself that the newly adopted principle is generally accepted, properly treated, and adequately justified by management.
SAS 34 P 3, 4, 6, 7, 10	If going-concern is a problem, the auditor should consider the need for disclosure of the conditions and effects of the problem.

5.2 REVIEW AUDIT RESULTS

Reference	**Description**
AU 311.11, 230.02 - 04, 160.11, 311.09, 311.10	All work must be carefully reviewed. The extent of review will depend on the qualifications of those doing the work and the circumstances of the engagement.
AU 338.01, 338.04, 338.05	Working papers should exist to support the key aspects of the engagement.
AU 230.04	The audit working papers should support the auditor's opinion.
AU 336.08	In audits where findings of a specialist are used, the auditor should consider whether the specialist's findings support the related financial statement representations. Additional procedures may be necessary in some cases.
AU 543.01 - 02	When part of the examination has been made by other independent auditors, the auditor must decide whether his own participation is sufficient to enable him to serve as the principal auditor.

5.3 FORMULATE OPINION

Reference	**Description**
SAS 31 P 22 AU 311.06	The auditor reaches his opinion by considering whether all specific audit objectives have been achieved through obtaining sufficient competent evidential matter. In so doing, the auditor is unbiased in his evaluation and considers all the evidence gathered, utilizing professional judgment, his knowledge of the business, and consultation with others as necessary.

AU 311.06 — The auditor will obtain an adequate knowledge of the business, which he will use in making judgments about the appropriateness of the accounting principles applied and the adequacy of disclosure.

AU 322.11 — Where internal auditors are used to assist in the examination, the judgments on key matters must be those of the independent auditor.

AU 336.11 — When expressing an unqualified opinion, the auditor should not refer to the work or findings of a specialist.

AU 328.13 — Where an illegal act is determined to exist, the auditor should consider the implications in relation to his reliance on internal control and the representations of management.

AU 328.14 - 19 — In the case of an illegal act, appropriate disclosure and impact on the auditor's report will be considered.

AU 504.01 — When an overall opinion cannot be expressed, the reasons therefor should be stated.

There are several specific situations where the insufficiency of evidence or other factors may cause the auditor to qualify or disclaim:

AU 331.01 — (1) Where confirmation of receivables or observation of inventories are excluded and other evidence is not obtained.

AU 333.11 — (2) Where management refuses to furnish a written representation.

AU 335.18 — (3) Where evidence cannot be obtained in support of related-party transactions.

AU 337.13, 337.14 — (4) Where the entity's attorney refuses or is unable to adequately respond to an inquiry letter.

AU 328.14 - 16 — (5) Where material illegal acts have not been properly accounted for or disclosed, or where their effects cannot be reasonably estimated.

AU 336.09 — (6) Where the work of a specialist is not sufficient to provide the basis for the auditor's opinion.

AU 410.01 - 02 — (7) Where the financial statements are not presented in accordance with generally accepted accounting principles.

AU 420.01	(8) Where generally accepted accounting principles have not been consistently applied in relation to the preceding period.
AU 430.01 - 03	(9) Where informative disclosures in the financial statements are inadequate.
AU 435.09 - 10 435.14	(10) (For publicly held entities) Where segment information is omitted or misstated.
AU 509.09a	(11) Where the scope of the auditor's examination is affected by conditions that preclude the application of necessary auditing procedures.
SAS 34 P 11 - 12	(12) When a question arises about the entity's continued existence that creates an unresolved uncertainty.
	Certain other special situations cause the wording of the auditor's standard report to be modified:
AU 509.09b, 543.03	(1) Where the auditor's work is based in part on the work of another auditor.
SAS 36 P 29	(2) Where selected quarterly data required by item 12(a) of regulation S-K are omitted or not reviewed.
SAS 27 P 8 SAS 28 P 4	(3) Where inconsistencies are determined with regard to supplementary information required by the FASB.
AU 530.01	The date of completion of field work should be the date of the audit report.

5.4 DRAFT AND ISSUE REPORT

Reference	**Description**
(No references)	

6.0 CONTINUOUS ACTIVITIES

6.1 SUPERVISE CONDUCT OF EXAMINATION

Reference	**Description**
AU 311.01	The first standard of field work requires that . . . . assistants, if any, are to be properly supervised.

AU 311.09	Supervision involves directing the efforts of assistants who are involved in accomplishing the objectives of the examination, and determining whether those objectives were accomplished. Elements of supervision include instructing assistants, keeping informed of significant problems encountered, reviewing the work performed, and dealing with differences of opinion among firm personnel.

6.2 REVIEW WORK OF ASSISTANTS

Reference	Description
AU 230.02	Exercise of due care requires critical review at every level of supervision of (1) the work done, and (2) the judgment exercised by those assisting in the examination.
AU 311.11, 311.09, 311.10	All work must be carefully reviewed. The extent of review will depend on the qualifications of those doing the work and the circumstances of the engagement.

6.3 CONSIDER APPROPRIATENESS OF CONTINUING RELATIONSHIP WITH CLIENT

Reference	Description
SQCS 1 P 7h	Policies and procedures should be established for deciding whether to accept or continue a client in order to minimize the likelihood of association with a client whose management lacks integrity.
AU 327.14	When the auditor's examination indicates the presence of errors or possible irregularities, and the auditor remains uncertain about whether those errors or possible irregularities may materially affect the financial statements, he should..., depending on the circumstances, consider withdrawing from the engagement, indicating his reasons and findings in writing to the board of directors.
AU 328.17	If the client informs the auditor that it will refuse to accept an auditor's report which is qualified, adverse, or disclaimed because of illegal acts by the client, the auditor should withdraw from the current engagement, indicating the reasons for his withdrawal in writing to the board of directors.

6.4 MAKE REQUIRED SPECIAL COMMUNICATIONS

6.41 MATERIAL WEAKNESSES IN INTERNAL ACCOUNTING CONTROL

Reference	Description
AU 323.03	The auditor may become aware of material weaknesses in internal accounting control (a) through his initial review of the system, (b) by performing tests of compliance, or (c) by performing substantive tests.
AU 323.01, 323.05, 323.06	Material weaknesses in internal accounting control identified will be specifically communicated to the client.

6.42 MATERIAL ERRORS OR IRREGULARITIES

Reference	Description
AU 327.08-12	In evaluating audit results, the auditor must look for circumstances which indicate that material errors or possible irregularities exist, and pursue these circumstances to his satisfaction.
AU 327.14, 327.15	Where the auditor determines the existence of material errors or irregularities, special procedures should be followed to discuss the findings with appropriate persons and to see that appropriate actions by the company are taken.

6.43 ILLEGAL ACTS BY CLIENTS

Reference	Description
AU 328.03	The auditor should be aware that some client acts coming to his attention might be illegal.
AU 328.04-09	In an examination performed in accordance with generally accepted auditing standards, there are numerous procedures ordinarily performed which may also identify the possible existence of an illegal act.
AU 328.10-13	Where the auditor determines the existence of illegal acts, special procedures should be followed to discuss the findings with appropriate persons and to see that appropriate actions by the company are taken.

6.5 CONSULT WITH APPROPRIATE PERSONS IN CONNECTION WITH SPECIAL PROBLEMS

Reference	Description
SQCS 1 P 7c	The auditor will seek assistance on accounting and auditing questions, to the extent required, from persons having appropriate levels of knowledge, competence, judgment, and authority.
AU 336.02, 336.05-10	During his examination, the auditor may encounter matters potentially material to the fair presentation of financial statements ..... that require special knowledge and that in his judgment require using the work of a specialist. Special considerations apply to selecting and using the work of a specialist.

6.6 DOCUMENT WORK PERFORMED, FINDINGS, AND CONCLUSIONS IN APPROPRIATE WORKING PAPERS

Reference	Description
AU 338.01, 338.04, 338.05	Working papers should exist to support the key aspects of the engagement.
AU 311.04	The auditor may wish to prepare a memorandum setting forth the preliminary audit plan, particularly for large and complex entities.
AU 311.12	Disagreements among audit personnel with conclusions reached concerning accounting and auditing issues pertaining to the examination, and the basis for resolution of those issues, should be documented.
AU 320.53	Information concerning the internal accounting control system may be recorded by the auditor in the form of answers to a questionnaire, narrative memoranda, flowcharts, decision tables, or any other form that suits the auditor's needs or preferences.
AU 311.05	The auditor should prepare a written audit program.
AU 333.01	The auditor should obtain certain written representations from management.
AU 337.06	The auditor should request the client's management to send a letter of inquiry to those lawyers with whom management consulted concerning litigation, claims, and assessments.

AU 337.10	If the response to the letter of audit inquiry is received in a conference, rather than in a written reply, the auditor should appropriately document conclusions reached from this conference concerning the need for accounting for or disclosure of litigation, claims, and assessments.
AU 323.04	If the auditor's findings with respect to material weaknesses in internal accounting control are communicated to client management orally, rather than in a written report, then the auditor should document the communication by appropriate references in his working papers.
AU 230.04	The audit working papers should support the auditor's opinion.

APPENDIX B

Format for Developing an Audit Methodology

During the course of our study of the firms' audit methodologies, we came to recognize and appreciate the extensive efforts underlying their development. To develop an audit approach requires many policy decisions. In this appendix we have attempted to identify those policy decisions that seem most critical. This is done by constructing a set of questions that underlie a firm's potential policies for each audit process step (using the framework in Chapter 2). In addition, alternative illustrative policies are provided. There are three for each question; they generally relate to the possible degree of central control a firm may feel is appropriate, and thereby somewhat roughly imply the degree of structure the firm may desire. For example, greater control may generally be equated with greater structure. Thus, alternative (a) de-emphasizes control; alternative (b) encompasses a moderate degree of control and emphasizes dynamic structure techniques; and alternative (c) places heavy emphasis on control and the use of static structure techniques. It should be recognized that the alternatives are for the purpose of illustrating the nature of the related questions. Alternatives (a) and (c), in particular, represent polar positions, and are not intended to be descriptive of a particular firm.

We hope that firms considering the current state of their methodology and possible future changes will find this appendix useful.

POSSIBLE POLICIES

Audit Process Step and Questions	Alternative (a)	Alternative (b)	Alternative (c)
IA—Accept/reject new client			
Q1—Should all potential new clients be investigated to the same extent?	Publicly-held companies should be investigated more extensively than privately-held companies.	Publicly-held and "problem" companies should be investigated more extensively than other companies.	All companies should be investigated to the same extent (i.e., "extensively").
Q2—How much authority should the local office have in accepting a new client; when is national office approval required?	Local office PIC has the authority to accept all new clients.	National office approval required on all publicly-held and "problem" new clients.	National office approval is required on all new clients.
Q3—What criteria should be used for acceptance or rejection?	Broad guidelines; basically a matter of judgment.	Specific criteria with allowance for exceptions.	Very rigorous criteria with no exceptions.
Q4—What form of documentation should be required?	No standard forms. Memo to files.	Standard form, but long-form vs. short-form depending on circumstances.	Standard form.
IB—Continuance of existing client			
Q5—Is formal effort required, or is this just "awareness?"	No formal effort is required. Just maintain awareness.	No formal effort, but criteria provided to help awareness.	Special formal effort is required.
Q6—If formal, when should it occur?	N/A	During initial planning.	Before engagement is started and updated before report is issued.

POSSIBLE POLICIES

Audit Process Step and Questions	**Alternative (a)**	**Alternative (b)**	**Alternative (c)**
Q7—Should criteria be the same or different than acceptance or rejection of new client criteria?	Less rigorous criteria than new client criteria.	Same as new client criteria.	New client criteria plus additional criteria.
Q8—Is specific documentation required?	No specific documentation required unless disengagement.	Yes—memorandum.	Yes—standard form.
IC—Terms of engagement			
Q9—What should be included in terms: • in the general case; • in special cases?	General description of purpose and scope; i.e., standard contents for all engagements.	General description of purpose and scope. Specific items in sensitive areas.	Specific description of all aspects of engagement, including fees, reports, dates, etc.
Q10—Should engagement letter be required on every client, each year; or should there be exceptions?[1]	Required in initial year and where terms of engagement change.	Required every three years and where terms of engagement change.	Required on every client, every year—no exceptions.
Q11—Should written acceptance be required; and, if so, can exceptions be allowed?	No written acceptance requested.	Written acceptance desired, but excepted in client refuses.	Written acceptance required—no exceptions.

[1]A fourth alternative would be to require engagement letters on unaudited work only.

IIA—Obtain knowledge of the business			
Q12—What aspects about the business should be considered essential to an adequate understanding?	General knowledge.	General knowledge in all areas; specific requirements in some areas.	Specific set of details that cover all areas.
Q13—How should the audit file be structured for this purpose; same for all clients?	No standard format.	Standard forms available; use is discretionary.	Standard detailed forms; used on all clients
Q14—What analytical review techniques should be used?	No specific suggested techniques.	Suggested possible techniques; user selects those which appear appropriate.	Standard set of techniques: probably computerized and classified by industry.
Q15—Should preliminary analytical review be required in all cases?	No; completely discretionary.	Required when internal control is being relied upon—i.e., not required where all work is being done on a substantive basis at year-end.	Yes, absolutely.
IIB—Choose overall audit strategy			
Q16—What should the overall level of assurance be; what criteria should be considered in setting it; and should it be the same or different for different engagements?	The overall level of assurance should be a matter of judgment by the partners in the circumstances for each client.	The overall level of assurance should be high for clients meeting certain criteria; lower for others.	The overall level of assurance should be set at a relatively high level and be the same for all clients.

POSSIBLE POLICIES

Audit Process Step and Questions	Alternative (a)	Alternative (b)	Alternative (c)
Q17—What criteria should be used to identify audit areas requiring more effort; less effort?	All audit areas must be audited to a minimum level with additional effort in areas determined to be risky.	All audit areas must be audited to a standard (higher than "minimum") level with reduced effort in some areas based on specific criteria.	All areas should be audited at a certain standard (higher than "minimum") level of effort.
Q18—Where differing levels of effort are required, what should the form of effort be?	Complete freedom to increase or to decrease or eliminate any particular type of test based on the cirumstances.	Must always do some analytical review and test of key items, although cutoff point for key items can vary. Other tests discretionary.	Must always perform internal control tests, analytical review, tests of key items, and tests of details. Only extent of compliance tests and tests of details may vary; they may not be eliminated.
Q19—How should the risk appraisal be documented and used in the audit?	No specific documentation requirement. Partner responsible for logical audit program in circumstances.	Documented by memo. Partner must indicate his response to risks identified.	Standard form used. If certain conditions present, specific actions, such as consultation, are required.
Q20—What criteria should be used to determine materiality?	No specific criteria other than partner judgment.	Quantitative and qualitative guidelines with authority for partner to justify departures.	Specific quantitative criteria with qualitative considerations which would cause a tightening.
Q21—What algorithm should be used to allocate materiality to various audit areas?	No allocation—separate determination area by area.	Algorithm with inputs of qualitative as well as quantitative data.	Statistical algorithm across accounts regardless of qualitative considerations.

Q22—How should preliminary materiality relate to financial statement materiality used in evaluation?	Preliminary materiality should be less specific and severe to allow flexibility in planning.	They should essentially be the same.	Preliminary materiality should initially be conservative and adjusted upward as year-end matters clarify.
Q23—How should preliminary materiality be documented and used in the audit?	Indicated in planning memo. Referred to when statements about the materiality of adjustments made.	Indicated in planning memo with statement of how audit planning affected. Amount of detail at discretion of partner.	Standard form for determination and documentation. Sets forth guidance for all areas including high-dollar cutoffs, minimum procedures, authority for passing adjustments.
Q24—Should there be a continuum of audit strategies to choose from, or only a few specific alternative strategies?	No standard strategies—only limits which can not be exceeded.	Three standard strategies: (1) heavy reliance on internal control; (2) no reliance on internal control; (3) small audit approach.	Only one standard strategy.
Q25—Is there some minimum level of reliance that is always placed on internal control?	No. Essentially a *totally* substantive approach is possible.	Yes—but can be approached through observation and dual purpose testing.	Yes—and related detailed compliance tests are required.
Q26—Are there certain audit areas where work must always be performed substantially at year-end?	No. Work in any area can be done at interim dates with some amount of bring-up work.	No, but only in the sense that bring-up work must be substantive and extensive.	Yes—certain areas must be done at year-end.
Q27—What criteria must exist to do work at interim dates; and what "bring-up" work is required?	No specific criteria—matter for partner's discretion.	Specific criteria provided for guidance.	Specific formulation of criteria which determine maximum intervening period and tests required.

POSSIBLE POLICIES

Audit Process Step and Questions	Alternative (a)	Alternative (b)	Alternative (c)
Q28—What criteria and algorithm should be used to select how many and which locations to visit in a multilocation engagement?	No specific criteria—matter for partner's discretion.	Specific criteria provided for guidance.	Specific formulation to determine how many and which locations to visit.
Q29—Is there such a consideration as an "unacceptable deadline" which would cause the firm to not continue with the engagement?	No—we'll do it whatever it takes.	There may be—we should recognize a potential problem and be sensitive to it in the particular circumstances.	Yes—if deadlines break certain criteria, we must decline.
IIC—Perform administrative tasks			
Q30—Should administrative requirements be the same for all engagements?	No—administration should be at the discretion of the partner.	No—but there should be sets of requirements for types of clients with appropriate criteria for classification.	Yes—using standard formats for various tasks.
Q31—Should time standards be established?	No.	No—but guidelines provided.	Yes—using specific formulas on an industry basis.
Q32—What criteria should be followed for accepting differences between budgeted and expected billings?	No criteria. Partner discretion.	Specific criteria with PIC approval of exceptions over a certain amount.	Specific criteria with PIC approval of all exceptions.

Q33—What criteria should be followed for assigning staff?	No criteria. Partner preference and availability prevail.	Guidelines provided. Partner negotiates with administration.	Specific criteria—partner has little authority.
Q34—Should there be a policy regarding the extent to which internal audit and computer facilities should be used?	Use if partner desires.	Use if certain criteria are met and partner desires.	Use if certain criteria are met; partner must justify exceptions.
Q35—What administrative techniques could be fruitfully used?	Little emphasis on use of administrative techniques.	Moderate emphasis on use of administrative techniques.	Strong emphasis on use of administrative techniques.
IIIA—Preliminary phase (of review of internal control)			
Q36—To what detail must the preliminary phase go, in terms of descriptions, observations, and assessments?	An overview level only. Purpose is to determine auditability and overall strategy only.	Overview level with observations and assessments of specific questions.	To essentially the full extent that the complete review requires; i.e., to the point of evaluation and compliance testing.
Q37—What techniques for gathering information and presenting descriptions should be used?[2]	Interviews and some form of documentation at discretion of partner.	Interviews and horizontal flowcharts annotated as needed.	Interviews, questionnaires, and vertical flowcharts containing narrative explanation of steps.
Q38—What criteria should be used in determining planned reliance?	No specific criteria—partner discretion.	Specific criteria provided for guidance.	Specific formulation required using standard format.

[2]A fourth alternative is interviews and questionnaires annotated as necessary.

POSSIBLE POLICIES

Audit Process Step and Questions	Alternative (a)	Alternative (b)	Alternative (c)
IIIB—Completion Phase (of review of internal control)			
Q39—Is it necessary to evaluate internal control in terms of detailed transactions and error types, or can a more global evaluation be made and used?	Can be done for major transaction cycles as a whole.	Can be done for major types of transactions taken as a whole.	Must be done on a specific transaction-error type basis.
Q40—Are there standard transaction-error-type sets for various industries?	No, and it's fruitless to try and identify *all* the things that could go wrong.	There is a standard general set which is used as guidance to determine specific types in the circumstances.	Yes—there are specific sets which should be adhered to.
Q41—If reliance is placed on control for one error type for a transaction type, shouldn't it be relied upon for all error types?	Not necessarily—a matter for auditor discretion.	Yes, as long as there is no clear reason not to.	Yes—always.
Q42—If reliance is being placed on control for one transaction type affecting an account, shouldn't it be relied upon for the other	Not necessarily—a matter for auditor discretion.	Yes, as long as there is no clear reason not to.	Yes—always.

transaction types affecting the account?			
Q43—If control is being relied upon for one account, shouldn't it be relied upon for all other accounts affected by common transaction types?	Not necessarily—a matter for auditor discretion.	Yes, as long as there is no clear reason not to.	Yes—always.
Q44—How should the extended descriptions differ from the preliminary ones; what tools and techniques should be used?	Additional information concerning specific controls being relied upon may be obtained if considered necessary.	Extended descriptions should be detailed in areas where reliance on internal control is planned. Flowcharts and questionnaires can be used.	Extended descriptions should be detailed and cover all areas. Flowcharts and questionnaires should be used.
Q45—What criteria should be used for assessing controls?	No specific criteria—auditor judgment.	Specific objectives set forth; criteria relating to objectives provided for guidance.	Specific format and criteria for each control objective.
Q46—What form of expression for the assessment of controls should be used?	General subjective evaluative statement.	Subjective evaluation applied to specific objectives.	Specific likelihoods expressed in quantitative terms.
Q47—How should the assessment, overall, be documented?	Whatever form is considered appropriate by auditor.	Internal control memorandum with specific contents required.	Standard detailed format—e.g., questionnaire or matrix.
IVA—Modify overall audit strategy			
Q48—Who should take responsibility for this step?	Senior with manager or partner review and approval.	Manager with partner review and approval.	Partner.

POSSIBLE POLICIES

Audit Process Step and Questions	Alternative (a)	Alternative (b)	Alternative (c)
Q49—How should the "final" audit strategy be documented?	By the planning memorandum.	By the audit program.	By standard format supplemented with memo; summarized in program.
IVB—Prepare audit program			
Q50—Should there be standard programs?	No.	Yes—with use optional; or to provide guidance.	Yes—with use required.
Q51—How much descriptive and administrative information should they contain?	None.	General description and some discretionary administrative information.	Detailed description and all key administrative information.
Q52—How should they be organized?	By audit process phase.	By transaction cycle.	By audit area.
Q53—How much detail should each step contain?	General—objectives-oriented.	Moderate detail—at least dates, amounts, and sample sizes.	Complete detail—task-oriented.
Q54—Who should review and approve audit programs and when?	Manager—before work begins. Partner—after audit is completed.	Partner—before work begins and after audit is completed.	Partner—before work begins, after systems work, and after audit is completed.
Q55—Is the program an intact document or a collection of documents?	Intact document.	Sectional, filed in sections of working papers.	Intact with a copy of each section filed in sections of working papers.

Q56—Must an historical copy be retained?	No.	Yes—as long as working papers are retained.	Yes—permanently.
Q57—Should inherent risk of errors enter into determining the scope of procedures?	Yes—it should have a pervasive effect.	Yes—but only in allocating effort across areas.	No—not at all.
Q58—Should the amount of analytical review work done be fixed or vary?	Completely up to discretion of partner.	Standard analytical review procedures part of preliminary planning; guidelines provided for discretionary use thereafter.	Standard analytical review procedures will be done at three points: preliminary planning, substantive testing, final review.
Q59—Should statistical sampling be used?	Completely up to discretion of partner.	Yes—for compliance tests; discretionary for substantive tests.	Yes—for all detailed tests.
Q60—Should sample sizes be determined using specific guidelines?	No—totally a matter of auditor judgment.	Yes—for statistical samples; no for judgmental samples.	Yes—for statistical and judgmental samples.
Q61—Are there certain substantive procedures that must always be performed even where maximum reliance is being placed on internal control?	No—not if audit objectives are otherwise met.	Yes—those required by GAAS.	Yes—those required by GAAS plus others.
Q62—What methods can be used to specifically relate the design of compliance tests and the	No specific method. Auditor simply designs tests based on his knowledge after review of internal control.	Specific logic process given to auditor for guidance.	Standard format to be followed and completed to make analysis and design tests.

POSSIBLE POLICIES

Audit Process Step and Questions	Alternative (a)	Alternative (b)	Alternative (c)
design of substantive tests to the review of internal control?			
Q63—What compliance tests must always be performed even where minimum reliance is placed on internal control?	None.	Observations plus some dual-purpose tests of transactions.	Standard set regarding completeness of transactions.
VA—Perform and evaluate tests			
Q64—What selection criteria or methods should be used?	Matter of auditor discretion.	Guidelines for high-dollar cutoff; representative samples matter of auditor discretion.	High-dollar cutoff formula and requirement for random sampling.
Q65—How should work be documented?	Program required. Remaining documentation matter of auditor discretion.	Program, working papers, *or* memorandum required. Some standard formats used.	Program, working papers, and memorandum all required. Standard formats used.
Q66—What criteria should be used for drawing conclusions?	Matter of auditor judgment.	Quantitative and qualitative guidelines.	Quantitative and qualitative criteria.
Q67—How should substantive aspects of dual-purpose tests be evaluated?	As additional compliance and substantive evidence.	As additional compliance evidence or substantive evidence.	As compliance evidence.

VB—Modify overall audit strategy and audit program			
Q68—How should final evaluation of internal control be documented?	Matter of auditor discretion.	Memorandum required to modify previous documentation and summarize final evaluation.	All previous documentation updated. Specific format for final evaluation.
Q69—What criteria should be used to determine when results are unexpected and significant?	Matter of auditor judgment.	Guidelines provided as a basis for auditor judgment.	Specific format and criteria.
Q70—Should an interim management letter be mandatory at this point?	No—only if in auditors' judgment a major problem must be communicated.	Recommended but not mandatory.	Yes—absolutely.
VIA—Perform and evaluate analytical review procedures			
Q71—What tools and techniques can be used in conducting analytical review procedures?	No standard set. Matter of discretion.	Standard set recommended. Tools available but not required.	Standard set used with standard tools and techniques.
Q72—How should these procedures be documented?	Matter of discretion.	Suggested format.	Standard format—required.
Q73—Must analytical review procedures be performed before tests of details?	No—not necessary.	Recommended except where impossible.	Yes—absolutely.

POSSIBLE POLICIES

Audit Process Step and Questions	Alternative (a)	Alternative (b)	Alternative (c)
Q74—What criteria should be used to identify unusual fluctuations?	Matter of auditor judgment.	Criteria provided for general guidance.	Standard format and criteria used.
Q75—What follow-up procedures are appropriate, and what criteria should be used for evaluating their results?	Matter of auditor judgment.	Criteria provided for general guidance.	Standard set and criteria.
Q76—What criteria should be used to relate the results of analytical review to the planned scope for tests of details?	Matter of auditor judgment.	Criteria provided for general guidance.	Standard format and criteria.
VIB—Perform and evaluate substantive tests of details			
Q77—What selection criteria or methods should be used?	None—matter of auditor judgment.	Criteria provided for guidance.	Standard set with format which is followed for selection.
Q78—How should work be documented?	Program and memo of significant findings. Form and content of working papers discretionary.	Working papers must be prepared but need not detail all items tested.	Standard working paper format in addition to programs and memos.

Q79—What criteria should be used for drawing conclusions?	Matter of auditor judgment.	Criteria provided for guidance.	Standard form to be followed.
Q80—What is the appropriate form of the conclusion?	Matter of auditor discretion.	Each test must have a specific conclusion. Aggregation done by overall judgment.	Each test must have a specific conclusion. Conclusion summarized in standard way for all tests.
Q81—What follow-up actions are required by differing possible conclusions?	Matter of auditor judgment.	Criteria provided for guidance.	Controlled by specific procedures for each situation.
VIC—Perform and evaluate post-balance-sheet review procedures			
Q82—Who should perform post-balance-sheet review?	Whoever partner deems appropriate.	Manager or senior with partner approval.	Partner or manager.
Q83—How should the review be documented?	Matter of auditor discretion.	Memo with standard minimum requirements.	Standard forms.
VID—Obtain management representations			
Q84—What criteria should be used for including representations?	Matter of auditor judgment (GAAS Minimum).	Criteria provided for going beyond GAAS.	Standard format.
VIIA—Draft financial statements			
Q85—What process can be followed to assure ac-	Upward resolution at request of engagement partner.	Independent review with upward resolution of all disagree-	Independent review with upward resolution of all disagree-

POSSIBLE POLICIES

Audit Process Step and Questions	Alternative (a)	Alternative (b)	Alternative (c)
counting issues are properly resolved within the structure of the firm?		ments—charge for national office services.	ments—no charge for national office services; automated "firm record."
Q86—What tools and techniques can be used in drafting statements and assuring compliance with GAAP?[3]	GAAP checklist provided for guidance.	GAAP checklist with sign-off requirement.	Interactive GAAP review computer program.
VIIB—Review audit results, complete documentation, and formulate opinion			
Q87—What requirements should exist for the engagement management review: i.e., who should do what and how should it be done?	Detailed review by senior; partial review by manager; business review by partner.	Detailed review by senior and manager; scan review by partner.	Detailed review by senior, manager, and partner.
Q88—What overall documentation philosophy and	Document everything once and only once in the manner	Document once and only once, but standards and guide-	Document all details in program, working papers and

[3]In addition to any of these, there could be an independent "GAAP review."

structure should be followed?	determined best by the auditor. Summarization of details allowed.	lines provided in key areas.	memorandums. Standard forms used as much as possible.
Q89—Should formal analytical review procedures be required for the final review of the financial statements?	No—can be used at auditor's discretion.	Recommended. Guidelines provided.	Yes—absolutely. Use standard format.
Q90—What criteria should be used to select the appropriate opinion?	Matter of auditor's judgment.	Criteria and examples provided for guidance.	Specific criteria and format required.
Q91—What requirements should exist for performing the independent review; should it be the same for all engagements?	Publicly-held clients require independent review; others do not.	Publicly-held and "problem" clients require independent review; others do not.	Same for all engagements—i.e., require independent review.
VIIC—Issue report and other communications			
Q92—What mechanical processes can be used to control the production process?	Docket with no other specific standard procedures.	Docket with use of automation based on updating prior year's report.	Docket with tracking system, maximum use of automation.
Q93—What post-audit meetings with clients should be required?	Matter of partner discretion.	Audit committee, CEO, CFO annual meeting.	Audit committee, CEO, CFO quarterly; Annual meeting
Q94—What criteria should be used to define a material weakness?	Matter of auditor judgment.	Criteria provided for guidance.	Specific criteria and format.

POSSIBLE POLICIES

Audit Process Step and Questions	Alternative (a)	Alternative (b)	Alternative (c)
Q95—Should material weakness and other significant communications always be in writing?	No—but documented by memorandum.	Yes—and approved by independent reviewer.	Yes—and approved by national office.
Q96—Should a management letter always be issued?	Matter of partner judgment and discretion.	Recommended except where clearly inadvisable.	Yes—absolutely.
Q97—What specific additional matters should require communication?	Matter of auditor judgment and discretion.	Criteria provided for guidance.	Specific criteria and formats.
Q98—Where there is an audit committee, should a formal report to the audit committee be rendered?	Matter of auditor judgment and discretion.	Recommended. Criteria provided for guidance.	Yes, absolutely. Standard format provided.
VIID—Perform administrative tasks			
Q99—How are staff evaluated and how are the evaluations processed?	Matter of partner judgment.	Evaluated after each engagement using standard form. Annual feedback and counseling.	Evaluated after each engagement using standard forms. Post-engagement feedback. Periodic counseling sessions. Affects assignments.
Q100—Should there be a required post-audit staff meeting?	Matter of partner judgment and discretion.	Yes—criteria provided for timing and contents.	Yes—timing and content based on specific requirements.

Q101—How should cost and billing data be analyzed; what follow-up criteria and procedures should be employed?	Matter of partner judgment and discretion.	Analysis required for each job. Follow-up matter of local office policy.	Automated for each job. Exception reports to PIC. Criteria for action provided. Engagement partners responsible for resolving.
Q102—How should planning points be documented?	Matter of partner judgment and discretion—points cannot relate to audit scope decisions.	Matter of partner judgment and discretion—all points are allowed.	List required in specified format.
Additional underlying questions			
QA1—How much integration should there be of the audit process into the other aspects and functions of the firm?	General coordination with other functions.	General coordination with specific points of integration.	Maximum integration of audit process with: Tax MAS Marketing Recruiting Training Accounting/information system International
QA2—How important is on-the-job training and how can it be implemented in the process?	Important. How it's done is a matter of partner discretion.	Very important. Guidance provided for accomplishing it.	Extremely important. Specific requirements in every engagement must be met.
QA3—What can and cannot be delegated by partners?	Matter of partner judgment and discretion.	Criteria provided for guidance.	Specific duties which must be done by partners are defined by policy.

POSSIBLE POLICIES

Audit Process Step and Questions	Alternative (a)	Alternative (b)	Alternative (c)
QA4—Should audits for large clients and small clients be done the same, and if not, what are the differences?	They may or may not. There would be a methodology for small audits, but it would be selected at the partner's discretion.	No. There would be separate criteria and methodologies for the two.	Yes, they should be done the same.
QA5—What is the firm's philosophy toward audit risk, and how should it be implemented?	Firm believes risks differ from client to client. Overall scope and documentation and review requirements should be adjusted accordingly (but not beyond GAAS).	Firm believes risks differ from client to client. These do not affect scope, but do affect documentation and review requirements.	Firm believes same level of risk should be assumed on all audits.
QA6—How closely should the individual auditor's actions be controlled, and how should control be accomplished?	There should be as little control as possible to foster individual initiative and responsibility. Style is discretionary.	There should be direction but not overt control. Control is achieved by providing objectives and criteria for guidance. Specific controls provided at certain very key points only.	There should be extensive control to assure quality and consistency. Standard formats and requirements should be used at each step of the process.
QA7—How should feedback about audit results be obtained and subsequently used by the firm?	No formal feedback. Respond to peer review.	Intra-firm post-audit review program with follow-up action.	Independent reviews result in recommendations within office for specific action.
QA8—How should changes in audit policies be communicated and implemented?	By updates to manuals.	By special form of communication—e.g., national office newsletter.	By announcement and training.

REFERENCES

Albrecht, William Steve, "Toward Better and More Efficient Audits," *Journal of Accountancy* (December 1977), pp. 48-50.

American Institute of Certified Public Accountants, *Codification of Statements on Auditing Standards*, Nos. 1-44 (New York: AICPA, 1983).

_____, *Statement on Quality Control Standards 1*, "System of Quality Control for a CPA Firm" (New York: AICPA, 1979).

Arens, Alvin A. and James K. Loebbecke, *Auditing: An Integrated Approach*, 3rd Ed. (Englewood Cliffs, N. J.: Prentice-Hall, Inc., 1984).

Bailey, Andrew D., Jr., and Daniel L. Jensen, "A Note on the Interface Between Compliance and Substantive Tests," *Journal of Accounting Research* (Autumn 1977), pp. 293-299.

Bedingfield, James P., "The Current State of Statistical Sampling and Auditing," *The Journal of Accountancy* (December 1975), pp. 48-55.

Canadian Institute of Chartered Accountants, *Extent of Audit Testing: A Research Study* (Toronto: CICA, 1980).

Committee on Basic Auditing Concepts, American Accounting Association, *A Statement of Basic Auditing Concepts*, Studies in Accounting Research No. 6 (Sarasota, FL: American Accounting Association, 1973).

Cronbach, Lee J., "Coefficient Alpha and the Internal Structure of Tests," *Psychometrika* (September 1951), pp. 297-334.

Cushing, Barry E. and James K. Loebbecke, "The Implications of Structured Audit Methodologies," *The Auditor's Report* (Summer 1984), pp. 1, 10-11.

Cushing, Barry E., D. Gerald Searfoss, and Reed H. Randall, "Materiality Allocation in Audit Planning: A Feasibility Study," *Journal of Accounting Research* (1979 Supplement), pp. 172-216.

Dirsmith, Mark W. and John P. McAllister, "The Organic vs. the Mechanistic Audit," *Journal of Accounting, Auditing & Finance* (Spring 1982a), pp. 214-228.

_____, "The Organic vs. the Mechanistic Audit: Problems and Pitfalls (Part II)," *Journal of Accounting, Auditing and Finance* (Fall 1982b), pp. 60-74.

Elliott, Robert K., "Unique Audit Methods: Peat Marwick International," *Auditing: A Journal of Practice & Theory* (Spring 1983), pp. 1-12.

_____, and John R. Rogers, "Relating Statistical Sampling to Audit Objectives," *Journal of Accountancy* (July 1972), pp. 46-55.

Felix, William L., Jr., "A Decision Theory View of Auditing," *Contemporary Auditing Problems* (University of Kansas Press, 1974), pp. 63-71.

_____, and William R. Kinney, Jr., "Research in the Auditor's Opinion Formulation Process: State of the Art," *The Accounting Review* (April 1982), pp. 245-271.

Grobstein, Michael and Paul W. Craig, "A Risk Analysis Approach to Auditing," *Auditing: A Journal of Practice & Theory* (Spring 1984), pp. 1-16.

Holsti, Ole R., "Content Analysis," in Gardner Lindzey and Elliot Aronson, Eds., *The Handbook of Social Psychology,* Second Edition, Vol. 2: *Research Methods* (Reading, Mass.: Addison-Wesley Publishing Company, 1968), pp. 596-692.

Kaplan, Robert S., "A Stochastic Model for Auditing," *Journal of Accounting Research* (Spring 1973), pp. 38-46.

Kinney, William R., Jr., "A Decision Theory Approach to the Sampling Problem in Auditing," *Journal of Accounting Research* (Spring 1975a), pp. 117-132.

______, "Decision Theory Aspects of Internal Control System Design/Compliance and Substantive Tests," *Journal of Accounting Research* (1975b Supplement), pp. 14-29.

Loebbecke, James K. and George R. Zuber, "Evaluating Internal Control," *Journal of Accountancy* (February 1980), pp. 49-56.

Mautz, Robert K. and Hussein A. Sharaf, *The Philosophy of Auditing,* Monograph No. 6. (American Accounting Association, 1961).

Mock, Theodore J. and John J. Willingham, "An Improved Method of Documenting and Evaluating a System of Internal Accounting Controls," *Auditing: A Journal of Practice & Theory* (Spring 1983), pp. 91-99.

Morris, William and Herschel Anderson, "Audit Scope Adjustments for Internal Control," *The CPA Journal* (July 1976), pp. 15-20.

Mullarkey, John F., "The Case for the Structured Audit Approach," Paper presented at Auditing Symposium VII, University of Kansas (May 1984).

Robertson, Jack C., *Auditing,* Revised Edition (Dallas: Business Publications, Inc., 1979).

Stringer, Kenneth W., "A Statistical Technique for Analytical Review," *Journal of Accounting Research* (1975 Supplement), pp. 1-9.

Sullivan, Jerry D., "The Evaluation of Internal Control and the Design of Substantive Auditing Tests," Paper presented at Auditing Symposium VII, University of Kansas (May 1984).

Turner, Jerry L. and Theodore J. Mock, "Economic Considerations in Designing Audit Programs," *Journal of Accountancy* (March 1980), pp. 65-74.

Wallace, Wanda A., *The Economic Role of the Audit in Free and Regulated Markets* (New York: Touche Ross & Co., 1980).